Take Five
The Five Elements Guide
to Health and Harmony

Biography
Pamela Ferguson directs the Zen Shiatsu programme at the Academy of Oriental Medicine, Austin Texas, and travels widely each year to teach at several shiatsu schools in Germany, Switzerland, and Canada. Trained mainly by Pauline Sasaki at the Ohashi Institute New York City, she is a board member of the Oriental Bodywork Body Therapy Association (AOBTA) and a member of the bodywork exam review panel of the National Certification Commission for Acupuncture and Oriental Medicine (NCCAOM). Her previous book *The Self-Shiatsu Handbook,* was published in several languages. As a former London based international journalist, she has written for publications like *The Times* and has published books on subjects ranging from Middle East politics, to the tobacco industry, to design and architecture. Born on a mine in Chihuahua, Mexico, she has lived in South Africa, the Middle East, Europe and North America. *Take Five* is her eighth book. It reflects her careers and travels.

Pamela Ferguson

Take Five
The Five Elements Guide
to Health and Harmony

Newleaf

Newleaf
Gill & Macmillan Ltd
Goldenbridge
Dublin 8
with associated companies throughout the world
www.gillmacmillan.ie

Published first in Germany as *Lebensfreude und Harmonie durch die Kraft der 5 Elemente* by Verlag, Stuttgart, 1999.

0 7171 2870 9

Index compiled by Helen Litton
Print origination by Carrigboy Typesetting Services, County Cork
Printed in Malaysia

A catalogue record is available for this book from the British Library.

1   3   5   4   2

For Bernadette

'The Earth has a natural system of interacting homeostatic mechanisms similar to the human body's.'
If You Love This Planet by Helen Caldicott MD

'The most determined effort should be made to eliminate those carcinogens that now contaminate our food, our water supplies, and our atmosphere, because those provide the most dangerous types of contact.'
Silent Spring by Rachel Carson

'*Luo ye gui gen* – 'Falling Leaves Return to their Roots'.
Falling Leaves by Adeline Yen Mah

'A knowledge of anatomy is essential for an architect.'
Michaelangelo

'The law of harmonic sounds reappears in the harmonic colours.'
Nature by Ralph Waldo Emerson

'Medicine developed to cure diseases caused by pollution cannot be considered an advancement unless we stop pollution.'
Zen Shiatsu – How To Harmonize Yin And Yang For Better Health by Shizuto Masunaga

Contents

Foreword

Using her highly readable style, her creative examples and her superb understanding of the clinical world, Pamela Ferguson has produced a rarity, a book that will not only be a resource for the advanced student of Eastern medicine, but also is superb as a first book for the uninitiated Western lay or professional person. For me, a visitor from the West, it served to both orient and enrich my understanding of theory and fields of practice in Eastern tradition. Unfamiliar ideas suddenly rang familiar through the rich personal and clinical examples that I could apply to myself and my clients. The focus on international issues and the relationships between the inner world of the body and the external social, political and physical milieu are other points of wisdom that derive from the author's wide experience in a number of cultures and countries.

The book forgoes a pedantic style, reading more like a novel, so I was drawn into a deep understanding of the life-drama created by the complex interactions between the five elements without always knowing how understanding had evolved. I can now weigh simple choices of what I wear or where I take my walks as important decisions that can affect my health and outlook on life.

This will be a welcome addition on my bookshelf alongside the classical tomes that may cover the same ground, but are not so much fun to read.

Beverly A. Hall, R.N., Ph.D., F.A.A.N.
Professor of Nursing
University of Texas at Austin

Foreword

The Five Element Theory is one of the basic concepts that formulate East Asian medicine. The theory is based on our observation of nature as an interactive force designed to interweave the different aspects of our life structure into an integrated, meaningful whole. In other words, it is the study of transformation and manifestation of the life force on this planet. In a broader sense, it is the study of how the universe operates and how we relate to it.

The Five Element Theory helps us understand how two or more supposedly different elements relate to each other and act as an expression of a person's state of being. Thus a physical ailment can be reflected in a preference for a particular colour, shape or food, usually containing the elements necessary to balance the condition. A physical condition can also be reflected in an emotion and a psychological and spiritual state. An experienced East Asian medical practitioner is able to pinpoint a problem that may exist on any of these levels and introduce what elements are necessary to remedy the condition and promote healing. However, since this knowledge is rooted in 'common sense', anyone can learn to apply the basic principles of the Five Elements in their daily lives. With this in mind, Pamela Ferguson offers a unique approach to studying and applying the principles of the Five Element Theory. The information is presented in a very practical and often humorous manner that everyone – the layperson as well as the adept East Asian practitioner – can easily understand and relate to. In addition, the chapter on case histories gives us a broad understanding of the practical application of the theory as seen through the eyes of a professional practitioner. Throughout the book, Pamela depicts the Five Elements as the archetype not only in medicine but also in culture and the arts. She uses examples of how the Five Elements appear in different forms throughout the world, whether it be in the language or custom. The theme running through the book closely resembles the archetype structure that Joseph Campbell explored in *Hero with a Thousand Faces*. You might even say that this book is *Five Elements with a Thousand Faces*.

Pauline Sasaki
Norwalk, Connecticut

Preface

Take Five will help you tap the roots of some of the most ancient systems of medical philosophy known as the Law of the Five Elements, a view of the human being as a microcosm of the universe. Lyrical variations on this theme are reflected in many cultures of the East and the West and the system is at the heart of our Western training in East Asian Medicine. We learn to diagnose ourselves and our patients according to the cyclical associations of the Elements, **Wood, Fire, Earth, Metal** and **Water**, and their respective seasons of **Spring, Summer, Late Summer, Autumn** and **Winter.**

There is something very reassuring about a system where healing involves you and your surroundings. On a grand, mystical scale, health becomes an expression of harmony between you and the cosmos.

On a local, practical scale, health is a balancing process between your physiology and your environment, offering you a fresh look at the links between the seasonal cycles and your body, your moods, climatic conditions, foods, your home, colours, rituals and much more.

However, the Law of the Five Elements faces mammoth challenges in the twenty-first century. We've lost eighty-five per cent of our rain forests and continue to destroy them at a suicidal rate of a football field a minute. As the late author William Burroughs once asked: 'What other species systematically destroys its own lungs?' Additionally, if electronic proliferation via computerised gadgets, portable telephones and laptops is capable of causing TVs to channel surf spontaneously or wheelchairs to spin around as if driven by a poltergeist, what is all this doing to our subtle life forces (**Ki** energy in Japanese, **Chi** or **Qi** in Chinese)?

Since 1950, our bodies have also been bombarded by 70,000 new chemical compounds, only a fraction of which have been tested for human toxicity, write pediatricians Herbert L. Needleman and Philip J. Landrigan in *Raising Children Toxic Free*, a fine work that also offers practical advice.

Twenty-first century health activism needs to link the environmental to the personal if we are to be true to the resonance of the Five Elements. To survive, we have to encourage more environmental medicine.

I was in Switzerland at the time of Chernobyl. Milk products disappeared from supermarket shelves. Farmers in Ticino (the Italian canton in southern Switzerland), and in Northern Italy, had to destroy acres of contaminated green leafy vegetables. Considering the widespread effect on the food chain, I believe those of us who were in Europe in 1986 cannot escape the long-term effects of Chernobyl. I maintain (though cannot prove) that Chernobyl accelerated the growth of a tiny, ill defined lump in my right breast into a tumour the size of an orange in 1987.

I believe my cancer was caused by a number of factors. Some of those factors include being born of mining families on both sides with high cancer profiles; living in heavily lead polluted cities; and, like many of my generation, exposure to excessive DDT during the 1950s.

I have since converted my experiences with all the factors prompting my breast cancer – and my survival through a mixture of conventional and alternative medicine – into vital teaching tools that help hundreds of students, patients and families grappling with cancer, each year. But all I have done is to transform the Law of the Five Elements into activism, with a lot of positivism and humour to match the times in which we live.

As a global instructor of Zen Shiatsu, I encourage my students to become conscious of environmental health wherever they live, not only in terms of the effect on their patients, but on themselves and their families. I encourage them to see no separation between the work they do in their private practices, clinics, schools and hospitals, and the work they do along with their patients, loved ones and friends, in society-at-large.

Far from being gloomy or pessimistic, our approach is uplifting and transforming. It blends health activism with the harmonisingly beautiful **Ki** philosophies and graceful movements of the East. Zen Shiatsu is a modernised form within Traditional Japanese Medicine (TJM). TJM streamlined, simplified and adapted Traditional Chinese Medicine through the sieve of Japanese culture over several centuries. Modern TJM forms continue to evolve through the experiences of innovative practitioners.

My experiences in the mid- to late-1990s with *The Self Shiatsu Handbook* published in English, German, and Russian, and my various media interviews and bookshop workshops on both sides of the Atlantic, have confirmed a large and growing popular interest in self-healing through the more accessible forms of Asian medicine.

Indeed, Americans rely on the media more than on their own physicians for health information,[1] while in western Europe, people consult their local pharmacists more than their physicians.

As I owe my own life to a mix of Eastern and Western medical systems, and to health activism, I welcome the efforts of Andrew Weil, Harvard-trained physician and well-known author of works like *Spontaneous Healing*, to promote the term 'integrative medicine'. Criss-crossing many ancient cultures of East and West, the Law of the Five Elements is truly 'integrative'.

Take Five is a natural sequel to *The Self-Shiatsu Handbook*, an equally practical, interactive handbook for families who seek more insight into their lives and day-by-day health needs. I also offer a new approach for students and practitioners of Eastern and Western medicine, especially for those whose interests in holistic healing appropriately include the environmental sciences, the arts, literature, architecture and anthropology.

Apart from formal Five Element texts by Asian and Western writers aimed at students and practitioners of Asian Medicine, popular books have been written in English, German and French on different aspects of the Five Elements, like healing with colour, or seasonal cooking. Mischievous cartoon characters Max und Moritz even have their own saucy version of the Five Elements in the German language.

For years, I have dreamed about the sort of book on the Five Elements I wished we had as students, but would be equally useful for the general public. The topic is perfect for a popular text spiked with case studies, eye-catching diagrams, fun cartoons and photos for a freshly visual approach.

When I started out on this journey, I had no idea *Take Five* would also draw on my past experiences as a global journalist, marketing and design specialist, as much as on my love of literature, my travels and my present focus on East Asian Medicine. I do not offer a traditional approach and I make no apologies for being a maverick.

Take Five is just the latest in what I hope will be ever-evolving interpretations throughout the twenty-first century.

Acknowledgments

My global friends, students and colleagues have all helped to inspire this work. I enjoy my discussions with Matthias Wieck, founder of the Tianxi Zentrum fur Chinesische Medizin, Berlin, and enjoy his deft ability to see the Five Elements in everything from his patients' apartments to herbal teas, to logos of the Olympic Games. I have been equally inspired by the Five Element innovations of my other friends and former students who invite me to teach in their schools, namely: Edith Storch (founder of the Shiatsu Zentrum Edith Storch, Berlin), Elli Mann Langhof and Heidemarie Kuhl (Shiatsu Schule Berlin and Dusseldorf), Wilfried Rappenecker (Shiatsu Schule Hamburg), Bernhard Ruhla (Dresden), and Erika Bringold (Winterthur, Switzerland).

My ongoing connections in the USA with my former Zen Shiatsu instructor Pauline Sasaki are always greatly energising. Similarly, my ongoing links in Canada with Montreal's Jean Lecomte (Shiatsu Ki Quebec), Raymond Ricard, Suzanne Ricard, Lise Ste-Marie, Elisabeth Reichel, and psychologist Claudette LeBlanc, Toronto's Tetsuro Saito (Shiatsu Centre), Kaz Kamiya and Nancy van der Poorten (Shiatsu School of Canada) offer equally invaluable exchanges and insights.

My friends, students and patients, come from an assortment of cultural and ethnic backgrounds. It is a joy for me to be able to reflect their eclectic array of voices and languages. To name a few of those who helped add their linguistic abilities to this work: translator Gaye Kynoch of Britain (Danish); translator Ute Schwarzer, originally from Hamburg, via London to the USA (German, French, Dutch, Spanish, Italian), Palestinian nurse Karimah Tarazi of New York City (Arabic, Spanish), and Austin-based acupuncturist Alighta Averbukh, originally of Odessa, Ukraine (Russian).

I would also like to thank Feng Shui consultant Annie Grey, designer Sophie Keir and Achromatopsia Network facilitator Frances Futterman for sharing their respective experiences and insights with me.

My global quest for an eclectic array of illustrations has been challenging. Tracking down Inuit sculptor Menasie Akpaliapik for permission to use his art in the **Water** chapter, involved weeks of emails, faxes and phone calls to Felicia Cukier at the Art Gallery of Ontario, and a network of trading posts, co-ops and store managers between Toronto and the Arctic Circle. My thanks to all of you. I'd also like to thank Hanni Forrester of the Asian Art Museum of San Francisco for the Japanese folding screens, Kathleen Ryan of the Philadelphia Museum of Art for Magritte's 'Six Elements', and June Botha of the National Press, Cape Town, for blustery views of the city's south-easter winds. I thank artist/acupuncturist Karen Greathouse, artist Jessica Higgins, architect Renato Severino, and photographers Jan Jordan, Nancy Scanlan and Marina Dodis for such spirited discussions about their work. My grateful thanks to illustrator Friedrich Hartmann for all the imaginative ways in which he interprets our requests.

During mid-1996, I moved my North American base to Austin, Texas to develop the Zen Shiatsu program for founders Stuart Watts and Annie Watts at the Academy of Oriental Medicine (AOMA). I also wished to work closely with three fine doctors they brought over from China, Qian Zhi (Jamie) Wu, of Chengdu University, Yuxin He and Guoen Wang, both of Heilongjiang University. I appreciate everything I learn from them. Special thanks to Dr He Yan Wu, acupuncturist and a great calligrapher, who provided the calligraphy for this work. My thanks also go to AOMA's Eve Berens, acupuncturist of Austin, and Erlangen, Germany, for posing for the meridian diagrams, for being such a super assistant and a great help with translation questions. And thanks to her father Professor Dr Hubert Berens for his insights on Goethe.

Teaching at AOMA has made me even more aware of how those of us in the West must learn terminology and concepts in East Asian that are basic to many Asian cultures, languages and idioms. This is only partly true of the Law of the Five Elements, because of the familiar parallels in Western culture, related to seasonal cycles, rituals and the arts. This is why the Law plays an even greater role in schools of East Asian in the West, than the East.

My deepest thanks also go to those super editors, Susanne Warmuth in Germany and Michael Alcock in Britain and Deirdre Greenan in Ireland, to a lovely translator, Ulla Schuller in Frankfurt, and to three wonderful agents, Edy Selman in New York, Ruth Weibel in Zurich and David Grossman in London, for being so supportive through both *The Self-Shiatsu Handbook* and *Take Five.*

And finally I thank Bernadette Winiker RN of Switzerland, who keeps me firmly rooted in Western medicine, and without whom I would not have survived cancer. This book is dedicated to her.

木

火

土

金

水

Introduction

East Asian Medicine/Modern Demands

Ideally, East Asian Medicine is about prevention, and not about curing symptoms or a 'quick fix'. Once upon a time, you paid your physician when you were healthy, and paid nothing when you were sick. This meant health was an on-going process of teamwork between you and your physician.

The Five Elements simply add the dimension of seasonal rhythms and cycles and their connections to your moods, clothes, home, rituals, favourite foods and much more, to help you maximise your health. Those of us who regularly criss-cross the schools of shiatsu between North America and Europe have helped Zen Shiatsu, and the way we teach the Five Elements, evolve through a Western prism.

I challenge my students on both sides of the Atlantic to adapt to twenty-first century demands, to the increasing array of computer-related problems, to the stresses of jet-age travel, unemployment, the proliferation of electronic gadgets, urban and domestic violence, addiction, AIDS, racism and sexism. In short, the sort of subjects that are absent from our traditional textbooks.

Indeed, with the exception of some recent textbooks like Carola Beresford Cooke's refreshingly different *Shiatsu Theory and Practice* of 1996, most of our textbooks are patriarchal in tone, as are most of the charts in our schools of East Asian Medicine, even though most of the students and patients are women. As East Asian Medicine is supposed to be about 'balance', isn't this ironic? Similarly, as of mid '99, the term 'Oriental' now deemed degrading, is being phased out in favour of 'East Asian'.

Unless we're very careful, terminology, topics and language perpetuate stereotypes in both Western and in East Asian Medicine. Edith Storch, founder of Shiatsu Zentrum Edith Storch in Berlin, constantly challenges her colleagues and instructors (including me!) to avoid the all too common trap of sexism in the German language. (In the German translation, we alternated male and female genders paragraph by paragraph just as we did in the German version of my *Shiatsu* book.)

Women's Health versus Men's Health

It's good to bust taboos in all our modern approaches to medicine – East or West. Sexism works both ways. During December 1997, much was made in the USA of a cable TV documentary[1] on men's depression, highlighting the experiences of media personalities like CBS TV's Mike Wallace, and William Styron, the author of *Sophie's Choice*. To date, depression has too often been dubbed a 'woman's problem'. Even the American Academy of Family Physician's widely distributed booklet on men's health, published during 1997, mentioned 'stress', but made no mention of depression, even though it hits one in eight American men.[2] Similarly, heart disease was traditionally considered a 'male domain', with women excluded from major studies until recently, even though heart disease is the biggest killer of American women! There is also a North American obsession with breast cancer, ranging from the glitzy cocktail party fund-raising circuit for cancer research at one end, to the noisy grassroot street demonstration and environmental protests at the other end. Yet prostate cancer gets none of this focus and attention, even though it hits one in five men in the USA, compared with breast cancer's one in eight women. Only very recently have men (like Michael Korda, editor-in-chief of Simon & Schuster, in his landmark book *Man To Man, Surviving Prostate Cancer*) begun to speak out publicly about their experiences. And similarly, men are traditionally excluded from breast cancer imagery and literature, even though one per cent of all breast cancers are male. Men who speak out about their breast cancer experiences tend to be lone voices.

Of course, these dramatic examples may not apply to you or your families. But they challenge our assumptions. They clear the air of some stereotypes. And they prompt us to examine health in new ways.

In general terms, *Take Five* will help you study and assess your family patterns of illness, or just seasonal variations in your own daily aches and pains, via familiar tools. You'll learn more about your health by diagnosing the balance of colours in your clothes closet, by diagnosing your home according to Five Element principles of Feng Shui. You may even recognise yourselves, your family members or your boss in *Take Five*'s case studies. Like medical detectives, you'll be able to put all the seemingly fragmented bits and pieces together.

The Five Elements also help us to re-examine some of the seasonal rituals, customs and foods that are at the core of many of our cultures, and can be at the core of our health, but are all too often lost in touristy hype.

I am reminded of the study done a few years ago in California on patterns of Japanese-American heart disease. People who remain close to their cultural roots and eating customs suffer far less heart disease than those who become thoroughly Americanised.

Five Elements, Meridians and Harmonisation of Ki

Take Five was also inspired by my innovations and discoveries, while teaching and working with the Five Elements since the early 1980s as a diagnostic grid within the Zen Shiatsu curriculum. We learn many different forms of diagnoses, involving palpating and reading diagnostic zones in the hara (abdomen) and the back, related to your meridians – or channels of **Ki** energy – your physiology and much more. We also 'read' the meridians in your posture, in the way you move, in your work-related problems or injuries.

The Five Elements offer us an even deeper insight into meridian imbalances. Not only is each element linked to a pair of meridians and their associated organs and systems, but to a comprehensive array of associations involving the colours you wear, your seasonal allergies or complaints, the foods you eat or dislike, your moods and even your choice of words and imagery or metaphor when you describe pain or feelings. Diagnosis is not abstract or theoretical. Diagnostic skills are honed through years of observation, touch, intuition and practice. Some shiatsu therapists base all their diagnoses on the Five Elements, describing themselves as Five Element Shiatsu Practitioners.

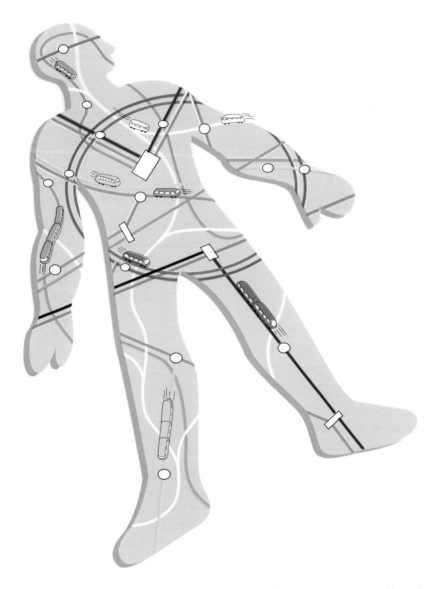

Meridians (Channels of **Ki** energy) line the body like a bus or train system, subjected to similar traffic jams and circuit breakdowns. Pressure points are like stops and major junctions. In good working order, they maximise a smooth flow.

My basic discipline of Zen Shiatsu, a modernised version of the ancient craft of acupressure – also known as acupuncture-without-needles – was formalised as recently as the 1960s and 1970s by the late Shizuto Masunaga of Japan. Masunaga established the Royal Medicine Institute in Tokyo to blend his insights as a psychology professor with his knowledge of ancient Chinese medical texts, modern adjustment techniques and many of the basic meditative Zen principles of centering and focusing. He established the form known as Zen Shiatsu by extending the Chinese acupuncture meridian chart through his research discoveries, and by teaching sophisticated methods of diagnosing and treating imbalances in the meridians relating to anatomy, physiology and psychology.

A meridian chart looks like an underground bus or communications system in the human body, and that's basically how it works. The vertical lines contain a number of acupuncture, or pressure, points (*tsubos* in Japanese), resembling bus or underground stops, junctions and main stations. Traffic becomes congested in some areas, and sluggish in others. The art of our work involves diagnosing and recognising congested or sluggish zones (known as excesses or deficiencies of **Ki** energy) in one or two meridians and their associated *tsubos*.

The acupuncturist uses needles to move **Ki**. We use a subtle blend of graceful **Ki** movements and stretching, involving hand, thumb, elbow or knee pressure on specific meridians and pressure points. I'm inspired by J.S. Bach, who once wrote 'all one has to do is hit the right notes at the right time and the instrument plays itself'.

The experiential focus of Zen Shiatsu broadens my experiential approach to the Five Elements. Of course you don't need to be deeply versed in Oriental Medicine to enjoy *Take Five* and apply it to yourself. Once you grasp the approach, much of it will be very familiar to you.

Ki (known as **Qi** or **Chi** in Chinese) is more than just energy, or life force, or electromagneticism. It's the substance that makes you tick. It's the difference between you and a T-Bone steak in a butcher shop. The essence of Oriental Medicine involves the harmonising of **Ki** (**Chi**). We determine the areas of stagnation, or the blocks, that disrupt the smooth flow of **Ki**. Blocks are dispersed by needle or thumb. Stagnant areas are stimulated.

Good health, or homeostasis, is free-flowing **Ki**. This is achieved not merely through a session with an acupuncturist or a Zen Shiatsu therapist, but through a balanced lifestyle, nutrition, exercise, meditation, consciousness and disciplines or practices involving all of the above. All of which express Oriental Medicine.

All of the above express the Five Elements and a sequence of **Ki** cycles flowing from one season, or one element, into the next, in a birth-maturity-harvest-decline-death-birth cycle. Everything to do with the Five Elements is cyclical. This is a reassuring thought if you find you are stuck in one element, or repeating serial-type patterns of behaviour associated with one element. The other elements are there to help you, to boost, nurture, move and act on your behalf.

Let's play around with some very familiar examples to show how Zen Shiatsu, the Masunaga meridians, and the Five Elements work together.

Five Elements in Action

Frustrated by charts and diagrams showing one-dimensional views of the meridians, I encourage my students to recognise the elements and their associated meridians-in-action in athletics, the performing arts, the martial arts, sculpture, or any other popular activity. The Five Element/Zen Shiatsu circle of **Wood (Spring)**, **Fire (Summer)**, **Earth (Late Summer)**, **Metal (Autumn)** and **Water (Winter)** offers all sorts of examples and here are just a few of them. (Associations are written in bold.)

Wood (Spring) See yourself in a **green** military uniform marching **crisply** across a parade ground. One of the meridians associated with **Wood**, the **Gall Bladder**, runs along the shoulders like military epaulets, down the sides of the body, and down the sides of the legs like military stripes. If you have problems with military imagery, just see yourself taking a brisk walk through the **woods** on a crisp **spring** day. Smell the invigorating freshness. Your **Liver** meridian will also get a good workout.

Fire (Summer) Imagine you are a **passionate** Flamenco dancer, castanets snapping away on a **hot summer** night. Your arms are raised overhead, exposing your armpits, and activating **Heart** and **Small Intestine** meridians, two of the four meridians associated with **Fire**. Now, to access the other **Fire** meridians, **Heart Constrictor** and **Triple Heater**, see yourself in a **rose pink** light. For **Heart Constrictor**, stand with your arms spread open, legs apart. Inhale, and on the exhalation lean back a little, so you feel a good stretch across your chest all the way to your fingertips. Slowly move your arms back and forth like a bird in flight. Now, bring your arms in and hug yourself, twisting (from the waist – but slowly) from side to side, to activate your **Triple Heater** meridian.

Earth (Late Summer) Imagine yourself cycling along a **dirt** road past fields bustling with **harvest** activity and an array of gorgeous **harvest** colours. After several kilometers, your legs begin to ache, but you feel terrific. Reach down and pinch the tops of your thighs (your quads) all the way down to your knees. You've just pinched your **Earth** pair of meridians, the **Stomach** and **Spleen**.

Metal (Autumn) Imagine yourself as a **Metal** masked fencer in **white** uniform in combat, clashing **foils** with your opponent. Certain thrusts and retreats activate or protect the **Lung** and **Large Intestine**, the **Metal** pair of meridians, running through the torso, either side of the thumb along the arms, and along the back of the legs. If you need to activate your **Large Intestine** a little more forcefully, just bob down into a quick squat.

Water (Winter) Dive into a **deep blue ocean** pool, nice and **chilly**, and on a **wintry** day if you feel up to it! Splash about vigorously. Swim several lengths, preferably the crawl for a while, and then back stroke. You are activating your **Bladder** and **Kidney** meridians, your **Water** pair of meridians, running along the inner and outer edges of your arms, along each side of your spine, through your bottom and along the back of your legs. Balance your vigour by simply floating on your back for a while, gazing at the sky.

Keep these action shots in your mind. Do as many of them as possible (walking, swimming, cycling), and just simulate the others if you have to (the Flamenco or fencing activities) whenever you can.

Easy Exercises and Meditations

A fun meditation is to do some deep breathing and then move from one picture to the next, seeing yourself in each of the roles through a filter of the relevant colours. Think of them as slides passing through your consciousness, awakening sluggish areas of your body, calming others, and telling you something about yourself. Don't rush through them – mull over each activity. Try to visualise, hear and feel each scene. Note your reactions. You will enjoy being in some more than others. These are useful meditations to do when you are travelling, or seated, or even bedridden for a while following an injury or surgery.

If you feel cold at night and are unable to sleep (which often happens when you are travelling), visualise the **Fire** exercises. Similarly, if you are too hot at night, visualise the **Water** exercises.

Energising the Five Elements with the Masunaga Meridian Stretches

The Masunaga Meridian system extends the twelve classical acupuncture meridians throughout the whole body, according to the **Ki** experience and research of the late Shizuto Masunaga. Masunaga, formerly a Tokyo University psychology professor, and accomplished in many forms of Shiatsu, developed Zen Shiatsu in the 1960s and 1970s based on his meridian system, stretches and advanced disgnostic methods. Zen Shiatsu is now one of the most advanced forms of Shiatsu practised in the West.

The combinations of stretches shown in these diagrams were developed by the author for her students, combining her experimental work with the Masunaga meridians and with Hatha yoga.

Practise these exercises in the morning to wake up your meridians in the Five Element cycle. Don't stress yourself if any of these exercises are too difficult for you. Just simplify or modify the stretches according to your comfort. Take your time. Some, like the gall bladder and liver meridian positions, can be done by marching around your garden or room. Others, like the yoga-like tree position for the heart and small intestine meridians, may take you a little time. To achieve perfect balance, fix your eye on an object or a flower, for focus. Do not arch excessively in the stomach and spleen position, concentrate on the lunge position with your legs and raise your arms to a comfort level. The other meridian stretches are quite straight forward. Don't forget to exhale while you are achieving maximum stretch. You can also do this sequence in the evening, to see how your stretches compare with your morning work-out. Repeat each position twice with your inhalation and exhalation. Take your time. Don't rush. Think of the elements and their related colours as you try the stretch positions, and make a note of the stretches your most enjoy and those you find yourself resisting. What is your body trying to tell you? And does this match the other discoveries you have made about yourself while reading this book?

You may also enjoy facing the relevant direction of each element (Wood/ East; Fire/South; Earth/Centre; Metal/West; Water/North) as you perfect these stretches. Create a circle in your garden and mark the directions with stones, with the centre for earth. It is wonderful to practise these at sunrise on a beach, or in your garden or your favourite room. Feel free to develop variations for yourself!

Masunaga Meridian Stretches

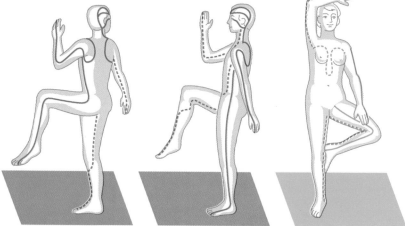

Wood
Gall Bladder Meridian (Yang) ───────────
Liver Meridian (Yin) ----------------------------

Fire
Heart Meridian (Yin) ------------------
Small Intestine Meridian (Yang) ───────

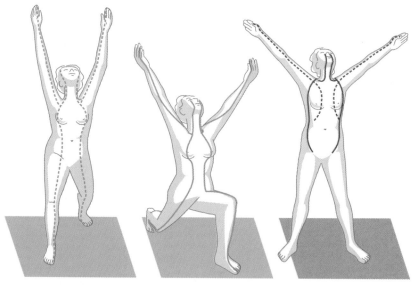

Earth
Spleen Meridian (Yin) ----------------------------
Stomach Meridian (Yang) ───────────────

Metal
Lung Meridian (Yin) ---------------------
Large Intestine Meridian (Yang) ─────────

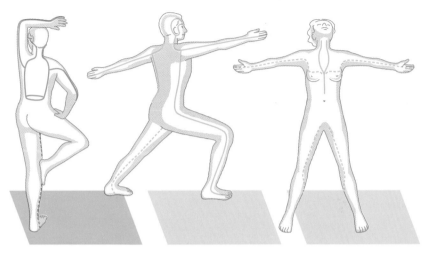

Supplemental Fire
Triple Heater Meridian (Yang)
Heart Constrictor Meridian (Yin)

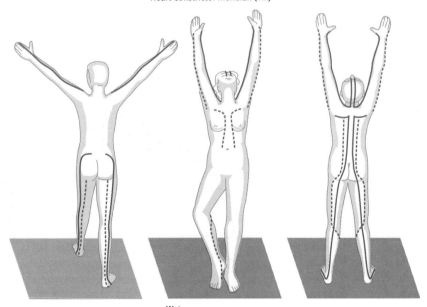

Water
Bladder Meridian (Yang)
Kidney Meridian (Yin)

Chapter 1
Touch, Taste
and See
The Five Elements

◀ Element Wood and Wind go together. Cape Town's mythic
and often violent South-Easter wind can whisk you off your
feet unless you're lucky enough to grab a lamppost!
(Photo © Die Burger/National Press, Cape Town)

When you got up this morning, why did you reach for a pink shirt without a second thought, matching it with pink pants and socks? Any problems with circulation? Let's see what's going on with your **Fire** element. A short time ago you couldn't stand the sight of pink and stepped into the world wearing blue obsessively. Any backpains that week? Let's have a look at your **Water** element. Last month you felt edgy, headachy and irritable on a windy day. You were experiencing **Wood** symptoms.

Last month, you craved sour pickles and yesterday you craved chocolate. What's going on? During pregnancy, you or your loved one chomped sour pickles *and* chocolate, so we would check both **Wood** and **Earth** for imbalances.

You don't like wearing yellow clothes? Well, OK, perhaps yellow doesn't suit your colouring. And yet when a cheerful little yellow table caught your eye in a shop window, you had to walk in and buy it for your breakfast nook. Why? Your answer lingers in yellow's link to the **Earth** element and reassuring overtones of nourishment.

Did you know that blue (**Water** element) is the world's favourite colour when it expresses the expansiveness of a glorious blue sky or ocean, where people experience a total sense of infinity?[1] And yet, in another context, a number of different languages share idioms associating blue with feeling down or a little depressed.

How do you feel after an evening of listening to the Blues? Certainly, the Blues jazz form incorporates a number of different musical expressions rooted in the African origin of dance tunes and worksongs during slavery, evolving into a form of oral history, or folklore, first documented in the 1920s. But the rhythmic framework for this storytelling (and not all of it is depressing) is the 12–bar harmonic layout. Interestingly, 6 is also the number associated with the **Water** element.

Have you ever thought about the origin of expressions like 'green with envy', or 'she has a nose for news?' Did you know there were expressions in several languages (German, Dutch, French, English, Spanish and

Danish – and perhaps more) associating 'gall', 'gall bladder' or 'liver' with anger? In the Five Elements, liver and gall bladder are all associated with the **Wood** element – and with anger! In German, *ist Dir eine Laus über die Leber gelaufen?* (literally, 'has a louse run over your liver') means, what's making you angry?' 'what's bugging you?'

The German expression *Ich muss mir etwas von der Leber reden* (I must get something off my liver) is expressed as 'I must get something off my chest' in English, and 'I must give air to my heart', in Dutch.

Green is also associated with the **Wood** element. According to the furniture outlet IKEA, if you like bright green crockery, you probably also like padding around in the nude at home! (*New York Times* Business Day, 12 February 1997).

True to the **Wood** element, many languages share idioms linking anger with gall bladder or liver. The German expression for 'What's making you so angry?' transliterates as 'Is a louse running over your liver?'

Have you ever Wondered about your Choice of Colour in a Car?

According to a Royal Automobile Club survey in Britain, people who choose pastel-colour cars are more depressive than people who drive brightly coloured cars, and people who drive white cars tend to be distant and aloof. People who drive silver or metallic blue cars are the happiest on the road, but drivers of lilac or lime coloured cars are twice as likely to provoke the rage of fellow drivers. The owners of black and red cars struggle for dominance on the roads.[2]

Would the same be true in North America? White, four-door cars (and not red sports cars) actually get the highest number of tickets for speeding in Austin, Texas, according to a survey reported by ABC TV affiliate KVUE 24 News.[3]

We all express our thoughts, feelings, moods and impulses so spontaneously that we rarely stop to ask ourselves why. Our choices, moods, feelings, obsessions, cravings and avoidances rarely happen by chance. They create patterns often confirmed by idioms in our languages and culture. All of these reflect some of the most ancient Eastern and Western medical and philosophical insights into human behaviour and the cycles of acute and chronic health problems, and how these are linked to the seasons, climates, pulses and rhythms of the universe.

The Five Seasons

In familiar terms, the elements and their associated colours, moods, climates and tastes move in seasonal cycles. Again, all associations are written in bold:

We begin, logically, with:

- **Spring** and its associated element, **Wood** and the colour **green**, freshness and new plants sprouting. But don't get too poetic. **Wood** is also associated with **anger**, and a **sour** taste!
- Next comes **Summer**, and its associated element, **Fire**, and a blaze of obvious colours, **red** and **pink**. Ode to **Joy**! But the taste is actually **bitter**. Now you know why that double espresso tastes so good on a **hot** day.

- Late Summer (or Indian Summer), is linked to the element Earth and a rich array of harvest colours – gold, orange, brown, yellow and khaki. Earth is also associated with your cycle, and a sweet taste. Now you know why you (or the women in your life) crave chocolate when menstruation is due.
- We move on to Autumn, the element Metal and to the stark white or grey skies we associate with late autumn, trees stripped bare of leaves, and a sense of melancholy in the air. The taste is pungent. Did you know white was the colour of mourning in many Asian countries?
- Our final season, Winter, is associated with Water and the colours of the ocean and ocean depths, blue and inky black. The associated taste is salty, which is why intensely salty foods (like kippers, smoked salmon, and rollmop herrings) come from northern countries with long winters.

Each season and associated element has anatomical and physiological associations linked harmoniously in creative patterns and supportive patterns (see Chapter 6, Case Studies and Cycles). Things go awry, resulting in illness or discord, when one element dominates or is weakened by another, tipping the balance in the whole cycle.

Weather and Climatic Conditions

- The Wood element (Spring) is associated with the Wind, with the way you feel on severely windy days, or in cities characterised by powerful winds, like Cape Town or Los Angeles.
- The Fire element (Summer) is associated with the Heat, with the way you feel in the heat of summer, or in cities or regions known for their oppressively hot climates.
- The Earth element (Late Summer) is associated with dampness, with the way you feel on damp days, or in damp houses or basements, or in climates or cities characterised by dampness, or when there is an excessive amount of fungus, or mould spores, in the air, as happens in Austin, Texas.
- The Metal element (Fall) is associated with dryness, with the way you feel in a dry climate, or in excessively dry regions (like New Mexico or Arizona) or in drought conditions, or in dry, airless rooms.

● **The Water** element (Winter) is associated with **coldness**, with the way you feel in a cold climate, especially in the excessive cold, or the way you react to really chilly air conditioning in the summer months. Few of us experience the excesses of the extreme north, of course. Physicians working among the Inuit remark on a winter cessation of the menstrual cycle and a loss of libido among many of their patients.

Contemplate your own physical or emotional vulnerabilities to the above seasons, and/or climatic conditions. Your reactions can reflect your inner landscape as much as the outer landscape. This is why many practitioners of East Asian Medicine seek diagnostic clues about the source of your chronic or acute problems, by asking about your seasonal or climatic preferences, vulnerabilities, and dislikes. Or simply by *listening* to you, your choice of words, your imagery.

One dismal February day in London a few years ago, I was called to the phone to talk to a friend of a friend, someone I had never met, whom I'll call Jenny. She was phoning from an island in the Mediterranean and sounded very tearful. During our conversation, the word 'damp' kept clunking into my mind like pennies dropping into a piggy bank. Jenny kept saying things like, 'It hasn't stopped raining for days', 'the house feels so damp', 'nothing seems to dry' and 'I feel so depressed'. I suggested she should fly home to her warm apartment in London and consult her family physician, and an East Asian Medical physician. I suspected she was suffering from a severe yeast infection, compounded by the seasonal dampness and the mould on the walls of her island home. She took my advice, and my suspicions were later confirmed. I also know from experience how homes built for idyllic Mediterranean summers can be miserably cold and damp during the rainy winter months.

Of course, not everybody reacts to external circumstances in the same way. Six college students could share a dank basement in London. Some will wheeze and cough. Others will feel gloomy and depressed. But others will hardly notice the damp slippery walls.

Windy Days Give You Headaches?

Certain chronic aches and pains are often associated with particular climatic conditions, like headaches in cities hit by seasonal winds. Cape Town's famous and legendary 'Cape Doctor' South-Easter wind comes blasting through the city in spring. Doubledecker buses topple over, metal rubbish bins rattle noisily down the streets, trees uproot. People cling to one another and to lamp posts to avoid being whisked across the street. Even though the South-Easter is said to blow the dust and pollution out of the city, it gives thousands of Capetonians appalling headaches and irritability, a prime example of **Wood**.

The Santa Ana wind hits the people of Los Angeles in similar ways. The city experiences more traffic accidents when Santa Ana blows. Like the South-Easter, Santa Ana is dusty and dry. The *Föhn*, a dry spring wind, brings awful headaches, tense, tight necks and irritability (all **Wood** characteristics) to the Alps. It blows in the mountains and creates heavy pressure in the valleys. Swiss physicians tell me there is a general sense of relief and release in their patients when rain falls.

My head would tell me when the *Föhn* approached in Zurich. So did my eyes (also associated with **Wood**). The uncanny clarity of light seemed to bring the surrounding mountains closer. The Swiss city of Thun, near Bern, gets the brunt of the *Föhn*, and is nicknamed 'headache city'. People who suffer from headaches in windy cities should heed the warning signs, do more exercise and stretching, swim (to ease tight neck and shoulders, a wonderful way of encouraging your **Water** element to soften or move congestion in your **Wood** element). Avoid fatty or rich foods, to avoid overloading liver and gall bladder. Eat some sour foods (but don't overdo it) and reduce computer work or excessive TV watching. In short, don't overload your **Wood** element. Try to avoid all arguments on windy days. That's going to be hard, considering how irritable you feel when it's windy and dusty!

Which Climate Suits You Best?

The elements offer various practical solutions. People with chronic chest problems, asthma or other respiratory problems often seek dry climates like Arizona's in the south-west of the USA. The **Metal** element is associated with the lungs, a dry climate, and the west.

In France, salt water spas have accelerated the healing process for people recovering from fractured or broken bones. This is a superb example of the **Water** element and its associations with the bones, and with salt.

The rule for one season may not apply to another, however. People who suffer from mould or fungus allergies often feel ghastly in excessively humid climates and should avoid them. The climate literally weighs them down, making them feel heavy, bloated. But there are also fungus-allergic people who feel equally miserable in excessively dry climates (like, say, Phoenix, Arizona in peak summer). The solution is probably a compromise – a more equitable climate with distinct seasons.

Two people with the identical symptoms may respond differently to climatic extremes, depending on the interplay of the elements specific to each person. A skilled practitioner of Oriental Medicine can make that distinction via diagnosis.

Take Five will help you discover something new about your creaky joints and aches and pains when the weather changes, your recurring headaches, your bursts of energy in certain seasons, and discomfort or misery in others.

Hopefully, these connections will help fill in the gaps in your health history, enabling you to discover links between baffling or recurring patterns in your ailments, behaviour or food cravings, past or present. You'll also discover links to your everyday expressions and idioms, the arts, classical literature and pop music, ethnic foods, herbs, dance forms and rituals.

You will remember things from your travels, recall past dreams, episodes, fears and joys, and even grandma's own remedies. And I hope you'll weave all this information together in the future for your own health and the health of your family and loved ones. With this potted and brief insight, let's pool all the associations we have discussed thus far on a chart before we dive into the historic and more detailed medical aspects of *Take Five*. Highlight words that jump at you:

Element	Season	Climate	Direction	Colours	Sense	Organ	Taste	Emotion
Wood	spring	windy	east	green	sight	eyes	sour	anger
Fire	summer	hot	south	red/pink	speech	tongue	bitter	joy
Earth	late summer	damp	centre	yellow/orange/ gold/brown	taste	mouth	sweet	empathy
Metal	autumn	dry	west	white/grey	smell	nose	spicy	grief
Water	winter	cold	north	blue/black	hearing	ears	salty	fear

Chapter 2

The Five Elements and Shifting Concepts

◀ Many northern countries share bonfire rituals to kill winter. This 'Fire Sculpture' was featured in 'Stockholm – Cultural Capital of Europe 1998' festival. (Photo © Lennart Nyström)

In Chinese mythology, opposing forces in the battles of gods and demons were once vanquished according to the roles of the elements. Spirits associated with the elements served as necessary guardians or protectors. In *Chinese Mythology, An Encyclopaedia of Myth and Legend*, Derek Walters emphasises the importance of the water gods and spirits, for a very logical reason: 'Floods have always been a recurrent disaster in China.' He also mentions that direction spirits associated with each Element are found not only in Taoism, but across Hinduism, and the different forms of Buddhism in China, Tibet and Japan.

Five Elements and Rituals

Some ancient Celts used to plant their seeds in blue cloth. The ritual – a symbolic recognition of winter hibernation – tested the ability of the strongest seeds to break through that blue winter cloth to sprout in spring.

Assorted variations on pre-Christian fire burning rituals to kill off winter and herald spring have, in some countries, become incorporated in carnival or *mardi gras* celebrations as a final fling before Lent. New Orleans and Rio's wildly colourful parades draw thousands of tourists each year.

Rituals are more than just excuses for street revelry, however.

Basel's *Fasnacht* in Switzerland is a very special affair and is historic with a modern spin. Dating back to the fourteenth century, the rituals of elaborately masked and colourfully costumed figures marching in time to fife and drum evoke past ancestors who return to the streets to scold and bless and scare winter away. Basel's parade starts at 4.00am with reveille, and each year brings new themes and floats expressing some bitingly satirical comments on local or national politics or events. After the Sandoz accident in Basel dumped tons of chemicals in the Rhine in the mid–1980s, *Fasnacht* included dozens of black clad and masked people marching alongside a float designed with grotesque imagery.

Political satire dominates Basel's famous annual Carnival (*Fasnacht*), dating back to fourteenth century rituals. (Photo © Pamela Ferguson)

Historic origins of many seasonal rituals offer us unique insights into the ways our ancestors celebrated them to ensure good crops, good weather and bountiful harvests. In short, to ensure survival! Exploding effigies and burning pyres of Zurich's *Sechselauten* send dramatic messages to winter each April – especially when snow is still on the ground. *Sechseläuten* actually means six rings (of a bell), and the ceremony starts at 6.00pm – appropriately too, as this is in the peak time frame associated with Water and Winter. Several northern European countries practise variations on the bonfire-and-effigy burning ritual. In certain areas, an abundant harvest is promised if smoke blows towards the cornfields.

To symbolise rebirth and renewal, or a victory of light over darkness or death, some Spring fire rituals in Europe were blended into Easter Saturday services, or celebrated in hilltop bonfires. Traditionally, in southern Sweden, if the flames of 1 May bonfires lean to the north, spring will be cold. If the flames lean to the south, spring will be mild.

The author (second on right) as a May Queen attendant in Portscatho, Cornwall. (Photo: © Pansy Coombe Ferguson, 1950)

In Maypole rituals of different European countries, people decorate their houses with green boughs and branches as a way of honouring tree spirits to ensure fertility, a lovely example of **Wood** and **Spring**. An earlier variation in Cornwall celebrates St George's Day (24 April), when 'Green George', a young man clad in green birch branches, is tossed in a river or pond to ensure rain for summer fields and crops. Honouring trees as the homes of spirits or gods has many ancient cross-cultural links, from Europe to pre-Islamic Arabia, and from Africa to Vedic and Buddhist India. The Hindu custom of honouring tree spirits is still practised in northern and middle India, when young, unmarried men and women are invited to dance around the branch of a sacred tree that has been planted in the village.

According to the Celtic calendar, summer starts in May, and the Cornish celebrate this in various ways. As a six-year-old in Portscatho, Cornwall,

I remember the honour of being chosen as a May Queen attendant one year. Some of Cornwall's best loved folksongs come from May celebrations. These include the Padstow Mayday song *Unite and Unite, and let us all Unite, for summer is a'comin' today* and the famous Flora song of Helston's lavish 8 May celebration when flower-decked townsfolk dance in and out of one another's houses.

Midsummer fire rituals (**Fire** and **Summer**) ranging from Northern Europe to North Africa, date back to early sun celebrations as a way of ensuring plentiful warmth for crops and animals. To symbolise the decline of the sun after Midsummer Day, writes James Frazer in *The Golden Bough – the Roots of Religion and Folklore*, many communities roll a burning wheel downhill. According to ancient Celtic rituals, the Cornish toss herbs into bonfires to ensure good seed, a ritual that has since become incorporated into the Christian Festival of St John's Eve on 23 June, according to Ann Trevenen Jenkin.[1]

Harvest colours, those glorious arrays of yellow, gold, khaki, brown and orange (**Earth** and **Late Summer**), are celebrated in a variety of harvest festivals, where, traditionally, the first fruits of the crop were offered as sacrifices to the gods, or to the reigning sovereign. Different religions continue the ancient tradition each time townspeople offer up the finest of their crops and fruit to decorate altar and pulpit. The Japanese Festival of Obon offers another variation, when the first fruits and vegetables of the harvest are floated across the water, and burnt with straw. Obon also honours the souls of the departed when tiny candles are floated across the waters, a ritual that took on even greater significance after Hiroshima and Nagasaki. I have celebrated Obon at author Kate Millett's farm in Poughkeepsie, upstate New York. After a huge harvest feast celebrated in late summer in one of the barns, we sent dozens of candles in tiny paper boats across the lake in the dark night. Millett reminded me recently that *fire in the lake* is the Chinese symbol for change and revolution.

Halloween and Other Popular Rituals

Halloween, based on ancient Celtic rituals honouring the dead, is an Autumn ritual, appropriate for **Metal** and **Autumn** – a time of parting, of separation, of mourning. Similarly, Day of the Dead *(El Día de los Muertos)*, a Mexican and Mexican-American version of All Saints and All Souls' Day of 1 and 2 November, is rooted in Aztec customs. It involves such elaborate decorations in the cemeteries that *El Día* has created its own distinctive art form. *El Día de los Muertos* is a far more flamboyant ritual than the quiet formality of placing flowers on family graves on All Saints' and All Souls' Day in the German-speaking countries of Europe.

Many cultures – ranging from Native American to Greek, Russian, English and Celtic, have practised planting rituals involving chants or oaths to honour Mother Earth, according to Barbara Walker in *Women's Encyclopedia of Myths and Secrets*. I now realise that I have been repeating a similar ritual ever since I had my first vegetable garden as a child. For as long as I can remember, I have always said a silent *Hail Mary* in rhythmic time to planting seeds in the soil.

As a child attending an Anglican school in Cape Town, how paradoxical it used to feel to celebrate all the festivals in the opposite season in the southern hemisphere – Easter in the autumn, Christmas in midsummer, Halloween in spring. As a result, I grew up with a keen sense of the ways in which seasonal rituals are practised in different cultures and adapted to different countries. I once stood on the banks of New York's East River in January, watching young Greek men dive into the freezing waters for crucifixes during the Greek Orthodox ritual of Epiphany. A far cry from the Aegean or Mediterranean of course, but very much of a **Water** and **Winter** ritual practised by Greek Orthodox communities in different parts of the world.

In the last part of the twentieth century, we saw some fascinating rituals during the opening ceremonies of the Winter Olympics. In 1994, children in dazzling red costumes skied down Lillehammer's slopes in Norway in a dramatic display of an ancient winter myth. In Nagano, Japan, in 1998, we saw massive Sumo wrestlers performing different purification rituals, stomping dark energy out of the earth and tossing salt in the air.

Finally, all the elements came out to play during Stockholm's Culture '98 festival. Sweden's extremes of Arctic chill and summer heat were expressed in unusual ways. Ice and snow sculptures celebrated winter in January in an ice pavilion. Frisky spring winds found form through kites, flags and air sculptures. A sea-fire and dance celebrated summer in June, with the combination of water-and-fire symbolising the interplay of rest and struggle. And during August, a multimedia presentation of 'wind, water, ice and the silence of the Arctic waste' was portrayed by choirs, dancers and percussionists moving up a spiral stairway of a glass column.[2]

Five Elements and Traditional Medicine

The basic human need to categorise and classify matter and mythology according to the Five Elements expresses itself in varied ways throughout the history of medicine. And often quite poetically so, suggesting an archetypal view of the human being as a microcosm of the universe. Health, or homeostasis as an expression of harmony between you and your surroundings, evolved through the prism of different cultures over many centuries.

Five Elements in Medical History

The earliest recorded medical references to variations on the theme of the Five (or Four) Elements are generally believed to have coincided in different parts of the world during the fifth century BC in no less than three philosophies: Chinese, Ayurvedic and Greek *Hippocratic Writings*. The trio helped to create the basis of our modern understanding of the term 'holistic medicine' during an extraordinary era of innovation.

Events straddling the sixth and fifth centuries BC produced some of the greatest thinkers and creative, scientific and engineering discoveries across many different cultures. This is the era that gave us Buddha, Confucius, Lao-tse, Zoroaster, Pythagoras, Aeschylus, Sophocles, Hippocrates and the Jewish prophets.

Bernard Grun's *Timetables of History* adds other gems to this era, including: the first recorded navigation of Africa by the Phoenicians; the use of the sun dial in Greece and China; discoveries by Greek anatomist Alcmaeon of connections between the brain and sense organs; Greek advances in water engineering, ore smelting and casting; and dam construction in India.

In medical models of the Five (or Four) Elements, the Chinese, Greeks and Ayurvedics offer different spins to the line-up of associations with elements, body fluids, climates and acute/chronic diseases according to the observations and experiences of physicians working in different parts of the world.

The Chinese included an extra season, Late Summer (known as Indian Summer in English and *Doyo* in Japanese). Late Summer belongs to the element **Earth**. It plays other roles in TCM and TJM. Not only is it the link between **Fire** and **Summer** and **Metal** and **Autumn**, but **Earth** is also the transitional phase between each season, and the centring or balancing factor within the cycles of the Elements.

Ayurvedic Medicine gave us another variation on the theme of the Elements, with **Ether**, Air, Fire, Water and Earth, and a different arrangement of associated categories. **Ether** is the most abstract, the highest form, the divine plan of the body. The **Metal** element of TCM and TJM corresponds to the **Air** element of both Greek and Ayurvedic medicine.

Individual variations are less important, though, than the resonance of the Greeks, Chinese and Ayurvedics in all recording similar medical models in the fifth century BC, rooted in their respective histories, philosophies and science, along with the reflections of their poets, epics and myths. All three cultures shared the basic view of health as an interplay of balancing factors between opposites, between internal and external landscapes, between heat and cold, excesses and deficiencies.

East-West Synthesis

The three systems later inspired other forms of medicine. Japanese Medicine continues to modernise Chinese Medicine. Tibetan Medicine involves balancing the three 'humours' (wind, bile and phlegm), and is a synthesis of Chinese, Indian and Arabic medicine. Traditional Arabic Medicine – itself a synthesis of Greek, Ayurvedic and Persian medicine –

incorporates four elements, and nine temperaments, related to hot, cold, wet and dry, and the four humours (blood, phlegm, yellow bile, black bile) of Greek medicine. Hippocratic medicine is at the core of Western medicine.

To challenge my students in North America and in Europe, I often read them a certain text and ask them to identify the source. In a crisply practical way, the text encapsulates the diagnostic approach of the Five Elements. The physician is encouraged to consider all aspects of a patient's illness. These include the environment, the climate, customs, food (and who prepares it), the patient's speech and sleep habits, body language (scratching, hair plucking or nose pulling), breathing patterns, body fluids, body sounds and symptoms of shivering or sweating.

For the most part, my students assume the advice comes from some ancient Chinese Medical text. In fact, it comes from *Epidemics 1* (Chapter 23) written in the fifth century BC as part of the Hippocratic collection of medical texts attributed to different Greek physicians.

Nature of Man in *Hippocratic Writings* discusses health and the Four Elements of Air, Fire, Water and Earth as a delicate balancing act. This involves the four humours of blood, yellow bile, black bile and phlegm, (*Himos* is Greek for body fluids), and their corresponding four seasons (spring, summer, autumn and winter) and four basic substances (hot, dry, wet and cold). The source of a pain or problem is described in terms of a 'deficiency' or an 'excess'. Such terminology is very familiar to students of Oriental Medicine, even though the Chinese and Greeks differ in season/ body fluid associations. Additionally, the physician who contributed to *Aphorisms* even describes the different effects of a south wind ('deafness, misty vision, headaches') from a north wind ('coughs, sore throats, constipation').

The *Writings* contain varying interpretations of diagnostic models according to the experiences of contributing physicians, but within a basic understanding of the connections linking diseases, seasons and climatic conditions. *Airs, Waters, Places* was a manual for itinerant doctors, outlining disease profiles of different cities, altitudes, wind directions and water sources. In short, the *Writings* offer us a variety of vividly graphic case studies that emphasise the art of medicine at the philosophical core of Western medicine, lost too often, alas, in today's high-tech approach.

Moving on from classical to medieval times, treatment of diseases according to imbalances of the humours and their corresponding temperaments (sanguine = happy — (blood): phlegmatic = lazy — (phlegm): melancholic = (black bile) and irritable/choleric (yellow bile) resulted in the excesses of blood-letting, enemas and urination observation and analysis, among other practices. Such methods remained until the sixteenth century, and are currently vividly displayed in the Museum of the History of Medicine at the University of Zurich.

Paracelsus and the Popularisation of Herbology

Swiss-born and highly controversial sixteenth-century physician and alchemist, Paracelsus, known as the 'father of pharmaceutical chemistry', revolutionised such practices by condemning the excessive purgatives and emetics prescribed by colleagues he dismissed as exploitative crooks. Supporting the 'Doctrine of Signatures', the belief that a plant's outward appearance indicated its benefits (walnuts for brain activity, for example), Paracelsus was followed by the likes of Britain's William Turner ('father of English Botany' and author of the *New Herball*) in the sixteenth century, and Nicholas Culpeper, who translated the *Pharmacopeia* into English in the seventeenth century, to help people find herbal remedies without paying huge doctor's bills. In short, Paracelsus launched a popular herbal warfare that enraged the medical establishment through the seventeenth and eighteenth centuries.

Paracelsus spoke of the human being – and of herbs – as microcosms of the world. His view of the (Four) Elements was very different from the Hippocratic and Oriental view, and very much that of an alchemist. He saw the Four Elements in everything, and believed that the essence of each Element could be extracted by chemical processes for healing remedies. Equally, he believed in the healing power of the vibratory frequency of such essences and colours, and said it was up to the physician to find remedies sharing the same wave length as the injured or diseased part of a patient's body.

Eighteenth-century and American-born 'father of physiomedicalism', Samuel Thomson went a step further. He combined Native American herbs and practices with European herbal remedies, and a belief that cold weather was the source of all diseases, which is why he favoured Native American sweat lodge therapies! He inspired other systems combining herbal with orthodox medicine on both sides of the Atlantic, eventually resulting in the creation of the National Institute of Medical Herbalists in Britain in the mid-nineteenth century.[3]

Natural Remedies and Alternative Medicine

Herbalists from Paracelsus onwards popularised herbal medicine by returning it to its roots as the basis of remedies people could find in their own hedgerows and gardens. I thought about this one rainy day in April 1998 as I strolled along the winding paths separating beds of healing herbs from different countries in London's Physic Garden. Set up in the seventeenth century to train apothecaries, the gardens are also currently involved in medicinal research with the pharmaceutical industry.

But then, natural remedies, at the basis of European medicine, are still mainly considered 'alternative' in North America, a younger culture. Family physicians who include homeopathy or natural remedies in their practice are not unusual in many European countries. Some of my colleagues in the USA are surprised when I tell them about *Kräuterheilkunde*, knowledge of herbal healing, and its practice in most pharmacies in Germany and Switzerland. If you want a natural remedy for your ailment, the pharmacist will mix something for you from large jars of herbs, herbal teas and concoctions. In Europe, people actually consult their pharmacist more than their family physician.[4]

Think about the herbal remedies you remember from your childhood. I remember the soothing dock leaves that grew alongside the painful nettle that frequently stung me in springtime on my way home from school along the cliffs of Portscatho, Cornwall. Now I know that I could have been helped by juicing and drinking the very plants that stung me! Also, a slightly bitter nettle tea helps to break up winter's 'phlegmatic superfluities', according to Nicholas Culpeper.

I also remember the sour, cleansing taste of wild sorrel in the springtime. In Cape Town, we used to gather early, faintly bitter nasturtium leaves for spring salads, and drink the pleasingly bitter *rooibos* (red bush) tea to cool us on a hot summer day. All of which gave me my earliest lessons in a few basic principles of the Five Elements.

Case Studies: Past and Present

Today, I view the assorted historic uses of the elements across many different countries as a vital way of helping us develop the art of the comprehensive case study according to patient, problem, culture, climate, source and remedy. In the formal Law of the Five Elements, modern students of Oriental Medicine get a wonderfully organised grid on which to hone their case study skills. I advise my own students to read *Hippocratic Writings* for inspiration. For a modern contrast, I advise them to read Oliver Sacks, best known for the filmed version of his work *Awakenings*. In his collection of stories published as *The Man Who Mistook His Wife for a Hat*, or *An Anthropologist on Mars*, Dr Sacks' brilliant mix of wit, creativity, compassion, observation and eccentricity converts the dry medical case study into an art form in which the physician's insight evolves along with the patient's insight. Or, in his own words, 'to restore the human being at the centre – we must deepen a case history to a narrative or tale'.

In Sack's tales, you end up knowing the characters, not just as patients with acute or chronic problems, but as men or women with unique lifestyles, talents, careers, joys, sorrows, dreams, environments, travels, relationships and discoveries. Dr Sacks captivates the essence of the Law of the Five Elements, although I doubt if he would see it that way.

Chinese History and Medicine

In China's political history, general uses of the Five Elements have see-sawed in and out of popularity. Different dynasties were once associated with different elements, in the same way that different nations were associated with individual elements, such as Egypt with **Water** and Persia with **Fire**. China's dynasties even drew up battle plans according to the Law. During a peak of popularity in the Warring States Period (476–221 BC) writes Giovanni Maciocia in *The Foundations of Chinese Medicine*, the Five Elements had multiple expressions via politics, cosmology, the arts and science, as well as in medicine.

Symbols of the Elements even found a role in burial customs. During a 1994–5 exhibition of tomb treasures from China (The Buried Art of Ancient Xi'an) at the Kimbell Art Museum, Fort Worth, Texas, I saw a display of bricks used in tomb construction during the Western Han dynasty (206 BC–9AD). Designed according to Han cosmology, the bricks were arranged in ways to protect the deceased's soul by reflecting the Four Princes of Heaven in Four Cardinal Directions, with associated colours and animals.

- The Green Dragon faced East (**Wood** element)
- The White Tiger faced West (**Metal** element)
- The Red Bird faced South (**Fire** element)
- The Union of Snake and Tortoise (representing the Black Warrior) faced North (**Water** element)

China (and Japan's) Four Princes of Heaven correspond to Egypt's Four Sons of Horus, the guardians of the Temple. Similarities can be found in Native American customs of dividing villages into four quarters. The Mayans have different birds stationed at the four corners. Navajo laws are represented by four sacred mountains.

The burial customs of many ancient cultures followed the elements, the idea being to return the body to its elemental state: to **Earth** (burial in a grave), to **Water** (burial at sea), to **Fire** (cremation) or to **Air** (chopped up and tossed to vultures, as we saw in *Kundun*, the 1998 film about Tibet.)

Contrasting Texts

Our major texts in English don't offer us a tidy agreement on the evolution of the Five Elements in Chinese Medicine. In *The Foundations of Chinese Medicine*, Maciocia tracks the ebb and flow of the law's popularity in medicine, through the scepticism of the first century AD to its formalisation within Chinese Medicine during the Song Dynasty (960–1279). In *The Web that has no Weaver*, Ted Kaptchuk claims that the Five Phases Theory was first systemised by Zou Yen (350–270 BC) and his followers, midway during an intense period of political and social change in China. In *Five Elements and Ten Stems*, Kiiko Matsumoto and Stephen Birch claim the most complete development of Five Element theories in medicine was in the *Nan Ching*, circa first century AD, which, in spite of paradoxes, somehow resolved the contradictions of earlier texts. Indeed, Matsumoto and Birch remind us that the Law of the Five Elements was not a doctrine, but a 'problem-solving device'.

Considering the philosophical cycle of the seasons and elements and their Zen-like analogies, it's also not surprising to learn that the term Five Elements is an inadequate translation of the Chinese characters *Wu Xing*. As Giovanni Maciocia reminds us, the character *Xing* goes beyond our understanding of the English word 'element' – to imply a movement, a process, a phase. This is why many texts use the expression 'Five Phases' instead of 'Five Elements', as in Ted Kaptchuk's *The Web that has no Weaver*, and Harriet Benfield and Efrem Korngold's classic *Between Heaven and Earth*.

Just as we understand the cycle of our own seasons being in a constant state of evolution, progression and movement, so too we view the body within its own cyclical processes, movements or phases. We use the term 'element' because it is familiar, convenient but it implies so much more in this context than in its literal meaning of a 'component', and goes beyond the alchemist view of Paracelcus we discussed earlier.

As in the past, the Five Elements have seesawed in and out of prominence in the modern era in China according to political shifts. Medicine is such a political issue, that under Mao, many aspects of TCM, including the Five

Elements, were considered part of the old feudal order. They were stifled in favour of the mass, fast training of 'barefoot doctors', the equivalent of nurse's aids, to spread the simplest of medical treatments to sorely neglected remote and rural areas. It is only in the post-Mao period of the past couple of decades that TCM has regained a role in medical schools.

Ironically, the Law of the Five Elements plays a greater role in Traditional Japanese Medicine (TJM) and in Western schools of Oriental Medicine, than it does in China.

Currently, China is a paradox. China has an ancient and revered medical system, but is a modern country with one of the worst human rights records to date, in spite of a veneer of social and economic modernisation and change and the emergence of a new entrepreneurial class.

It's still common in China for baby girls born in rural areas to be discarded or dumped. Although the practice is less stringent in the cities, the cultural preference for boys results in a huge imbalance in the number of boy children, and the elimination of baby girls 'on a massive scale', according to a report co-written by demographer Jiali Li and anthropologist Susan Greenhalgh from the University of California at Irvine.[5]

China also has one of the worst records to date of environmental pollution, with seven of the world's most polluted rivers, according to the World Bank. During 1998, weekly air quality reports from China's major cities recorded the highest levels of pollutants in the world (mainly caused by coal) resulting in some 178,000 premature deaths a year, and an asthma rate of five per cent around factories. Official statistics are being released for the first time, to boost efforts to combat the problem, including a search for alternatives to coal, the closing down of antiquated factories (as happened in Eastern Europe after 1989), and a 1999 ban on leaded gas.[6]

However, cigarette smoking, considered a major contributor to pollution in China, has one of the world's fastest growth rates, stimulated by a state-controlled industry.[7] The number of smokers in China exceeds the total population of the USA. Two-thirds of men smoke, lung cancer rates are soaring and China has the highest per capita number of smoking-related deaths in the world, (one in four people). Hopefully, China's process of 'opening up' may spur more enlightenment during the twenty-first century.

To date, medical doctors who spoke out on environmental and public health issues have been treated like any other dissident. Medical schools are still organised along strictly hierarchical lines, leaving little room for challenge.

Shortly after the Tiananmen Square massacre, I was teaching in Hamburg and experienced an interesting situation. Some of my students approached me as they were concerned about a young Chinese friend and dissident who had recently arrived in the city. 'He's experiencing constant ringing in his ears,' they said. 'We'd like to pay for him to come to you for a shiatsu session.' Whenever I share this story with my classes as a lesson in diagnosis, I get a barrage of responses about possible imbalances in his **Water** element and the most effective meridians and combination of points they would have used in such a situation.

'Wait,' I tell them. 'You're looking at the wrong end of the problem! My first question was, "Does the young man have any fellow dissident Chinese students in Hamburg?" His German friends said no, he was very much alone.

"Ah," I replied, "there's your answer. He's missing his roots. Don't waste your money on shiatsu. Buy him a return ticket to Paris so he can spend a little time with other Chinese dissidents and student groups."' They did just that. Off he went on the train to Paris. The ringing in his ears stopped.

East versus West versus East

Colonisation had an impact on the practice of traditional forms of medicine in many Asian countries, and on pre-Mao China. The influence of Western doctors and European-style medical schools and hospitals has been profound, often in the name of so-called 'civilisation' or modernising 'primitive and backward' methods. It was interesting to read physician

Adeline Yen Mah's *Falling Leaves*. Her personal story and tragic childhood reflect a twilight zone between ancient Chinese traditions and customs and a thoroughly Western education in Shanghai, including her Western medical training and practice in Britain and the USA.

Several TJM practices (including the form of shiatsu practised by blind therapists) were outlawed during the American occupation of Japan following World War II, only to be revived and expanded along with the technological advances from the 1960s onwards. Modern Japan offers many shiatsu forms, some of which are taught in the West, and continue to evolve through the gifted hands of internationally respected instructors like Pauline Sasaki of Connecticut, and through the Western experiences of pioneering instructors from Japan, such as Tet Saito and Kaz Kamiya, now of Toronto, Ontario, Canada. This has had some interesting repercussions. I heard recently that Ohashi, one of my former instructors who helped to popularise shiatsu in the West from the 1970s onwards, recently gave classes in *English* in his native Japan, because his new work would not be acceptable in his own tongue.

I was surprised to be invited to teach Zen Shiatsu in Kuala Lumpur, Singapore and Hong Kong, only to be told that many traditional medical practices which were stifled by colonialism are being re-introduced via their spreading popularity in the West. No amount of colonisation could stamp the Five Elements out of Asian cultures and cuisines, however. Because of this, in culture and in medicine, the Five Elements offer something of a refreshment station on a two-way bridge between East and West.

Chapter 3

Movement in Stillness and Stillness in Movement

◀ An unusual expression of the Water element and Winter in the Jukkasjärvi Ice Hotel of Swedish Lapland, exhibited during Stockholm 'Cultural Capital of Europe 1998' Festival. (Photo © Jan Jordan)

Yin and Yang

One of the most beautiful Zen expressions I incorporate into my teaching, is: movement in stillness and stillness in movement. Not only does it express the essence of the harmonising and graceful form of Zen Shiatsu, but it is also an expression of *Yang* (Movement) and *Yin* (Stillness), not as opposites, but as complements.

The Taoist Yin/Yang theory of complementary opposites is basic to our understanding of Chinese philosophy and its expression through Oriental Medicine. The theory also predates the Five Elements by several centuries. The earliest references to Yin and Yang date back to around 1000 BC during the Zhou Dynasty, several centuries before the earliest medical references to the Five Elements, according to Giovanni Maciocia. General references to the Five Elements appeared several centuries earlier, however. The development of Yin/Yang and the Five Elements as scientific theories evolved out of the same philosophical school. This makes a lot of sense. Yin and Yang play roles within the cyclical movement of the Five Elements, and within each Element.

The Five Elements simply expand the Yin/Yang concept. There is no convenient line dividing Yin from Yang. There are no absolutes. No 'either or'. Nothing is static. There is cyclical movement. There is transformation from one into the other (as night into day), just as there is transformation within the cycles of the Five Elements (as in **Winter/Yin** evolving into **Spring/Yang**).

Exposure to the fluidity of Yin and Yang in assorted manifestations in nature and medicine helps broaden our view beyond the sort of tightly logical approach (A = A) we generally associate with Aristotelian and Cartesian thinking in the West. Added to this, Zen also has a way of exploding our preconceived, logical (thus comfortable) views. I sometimes illustrate this in my classes by asking two students to sit back to back. 'Look to the right,' I tell them. They look in opposite directions.

Life is an ongoing interplay between Yin and Yang. Think of the opposites we encounter in our daily lives. Moon and Sun, Night and Day, Cold and Hot, Stillness and Movement, Matter and Energy, Dark and Bright. None of these are absolutes. Shade offers cool, Yin relief to a blisteringly hot Yang day. A clear bright moon illuminates your path and gives a Yang quality to a Yin night. Those of us who prefer politically correct terminology avoid including the feminine and masculine principles often associated with Yin and Yang, because of a misuse of stereotypes in the past, for example: Yin = female = dark = negative = weak versus Yang = male = light = positive = strong. I usually blow this concept by reminding my students that, in the Latin languages, sun is masculine and moon is feminine; but in German, sun is feminine and moon is masculine!

Electricity depends on negative and positive charges. You line up your batteries in your torch or portable radio according to the 'plus' and 'minus' signs. When you leave your car lights on overnight, your solution is to jump-start your battery by attaching cables with a black (Yin) clip and a red (Yang) clip. Our bodies are full of Yin/Yang examples. Think of your Ph balance. Think of exhalation and inhalation, contraction and expansion. The front of your body is Yin, the back is Yang.

In Germany, sun is female and moon is male, but in Italy, sun is male and moon is female!

Contemplate the Yin/Yang symbol for a moment. It is not linear and divisive or separating, but circular, progressive and revolving. There is always a light (Yang) circle within the dark Yin half, and likewise, a dark (Yin) circle within the light Yang half.

Each of the Five Elements has Yin and Yang aspects. Seasonally, the circles within the Five Elements cycle move from their relative Yang **(Spring/ Summer)** or extrovert, outward, noisy phases, to their relative Yin **(Autumn/Winter)** or introvert, inward, hibernating phases, with a balancing link easing Yang into Yin in **Late Summer**. With everything being relative, you will have Yin and Yang aspects of each season, and each day in each season! The Law of the Five Elements expands this grid with a vivid patchwork of seasons, colours, sounds, tastes and foods.

The Elements and Your Meridians

In Shiatsu we work within a symmetrical grid of six Yin/Yang pairs of meridians, or channels of **Ki** energy, lined up vertically in the body like a bus or train system, dotted with pressure or acupuncture points like bus stops, and main stations. The meridians relate to anatomy, physiology, psychology – and a lot more.

The Yin meridians run from Earth to Heaven (feet to head), and the Yang meridians run from Heaven to Earth (head to feet). Each element has a set of meridians. Through our diagnostic work, of which the Five Elements is one of the most comprehensive approaches, we determine which meridians are on overload, which are sluggish, and why.

In Zen Shiatsu, the elements and their meridian partners cover a number of different functions, not just the obvious organs or systems of the same name. There's a simple way of explaining the differences between Yin and Yang organs. Yin organs are dense (heart, lung, kidney); Yang organs are hollow and transporting (large intestine, small intestine, bladder).

With this in mind, let's expand our previous charts:

Element:	Wood
Season:	Spring
Climate:	Windy
Direction:	East
Meridians:	Gall Bladder **(Yang)**; Liver **(Yin)**
Body Part:	Muscles, tendons, joints
Sense Organ:	Eyes
Sense:	Sight
Fluid:	Tears
Emotion:	Anger
Behaviour Patterns:	Decision, indecision, control
Sound:	Shouting
Taste:	Sour

Brief summary: **Wood** is about new growth and change and the burst of spring, all of which involves a lot of energy and movement. It's the Element to examine when you suddenly crave sour pickles or wear an enormous amount of green. Stiff, tight muscles and joints also reflect **Wood** imbalances, as do eyestrain and migraines, especially from computer overload. The **(Yang) Gall Bladder** meridian and its **(Yin)** partner the **Liver** meridian don't just control the functions of their related organs, but also control the distribution and storage of nourishment in your body, and much more. The **Liver** meridian also controls prostate and testicular problems. There is lots of testosterone in the **Wood** zone. Trial lawyers are supposed to have thirty per cent more testosterone than the average man in the USA. **Wood** involves high pressure executive planning and decisions, the way you handle aggression, angry outbursts **(Liver)** and smouldering anger turned inward **(Gall Bladder)** We also come across lots of Wall Street executives, generals and top politicians – and trial lawyers – in the **Wood** zone.

Element:	Fire
Climate:	Hot
Direction:	South
Meridians:	Small Intestine **(Yang)**; Heart **(Yin)** **(Absolute Fire)** Triple Heater **(Yang)**; Heart Constrictor **(Yin)** **(Supplemental Fire)**
Body Part:	Blood vessels
Sense Organ:	Tongue
Sense:	Speech
Fluid:	Sweat
Emotion:	Joy
Behaviour Patterns:	Nervous giggling
Sound:	Laughter
Taste:	Bitter

Brief Summary: **Fire** is about the joy of hot, passionate summer days and luscious deep red strawberries, and sipping campari in a lingering sunset. Laughter and joy are good for the immune system, but **Fire** imbalances show up in people who laugh or giggle obsessively even when there is nothing to laugh about. **Fire** imbalances are also revealed in many speech problems, or when you are tongue-tied.

The two pairs of **Fire** meridians play different roles. In the **Absolute Fire** camp, the **(Yin) Heart** meridian not only governs your physical and emotional heart, but the way you process and absorb the external world through all your senses. Its **(Yang)** partner, **Small Intestine** meridian, controls the way you absorb and assimilate your food, and the way you absorb and assimilate facts. So, too much cramming of facts (and junk foods) prior to an exam can throw the **Small Intestine**!

The **Supplemental Fire** camp is all about the systems that protect you. The **(Yin) Heart Constrictor**, also known as the **Pericardium**, protects your heart physically and emotionally, controls your circulation and your sleep patterns, and psychological aspects of your personal and sex life. It gets thrown out of whack when you go through a divorce. I often dub it **the divorce meridian.**

Its **(Yang)** partner, the **Triple Heater** (or **Triple Warmer**) is your body's thermostat. It also controls your lymph and immune systems. It helps you adapt to change, especially when you are travelling long distances and from one climate, or time zone, to the next. It's my favourite in-flight meridian, because it helps prevent jet-lag. So I nickname it **the travellers' meridian.**

Element:	**Earth**
Climate:	Damp, humid
Direction:	Centre
Meridians:	Stomach **(Yang)**; Spleen **(Yin)**
Body Part:	Flesh
Sense Organ:	Mouth
Sense:	Taste
Fluid:	Saliva
Emotion:	Compassion/empathy
Behaviour Patterns:	Obsessive, smothering, overprotective
Sound:	Sing-song voice
Taste:	Sweet

Brief Summary: **Earth** is about nourishment and digestion, nurturing and reproduction, and your menstrual and mood cycles. **Earth** is also about eating disorders (over-eating or anorexia) on a grand scale. But on a cyclical scale, it relates to those moments when you crave desserts and sweets. Earth is about compassion and empathy, but there's also a danger of over-parenting and smothering here too. The **(Yang) Stomach Meridian** does not just control your stomach organ, but your oesophagus, and also the function of the uterus, breasts and lactation. Your relationships with your parents and children are often reflected here. In fact, the **Stomach Meridian** runs down the milk line in the torso of animals, linking the line of teats so easily seen in female dogs or cats mothering their young. The **(Yin) Spleen Meridian** not only controls the function of the spleen and pancreas organs, and your digestive juices, but your ovaries. The meridian also runs through the upper outer quadrant of the breasts, where most tumours occur, so it also plays a role in breast function.

The **Spleen Meridian** also controls memory and thinking. Too much studying and too little exercise throw this meridian out of balance, as does an obsessive idea or fixation, known appropriately in German as *einen Spleen haben.*

Element:	Metal
Colours:	White, grey
Climate:	Dry
Direction:	West
Meridians:	Large intestine (**Yang**); Lung (**Yin**)
Body Part:	Skin
Sense Organ:	Nose
Sense:	Smell
Fluid:	Mucus
Emotion:	Grief, melancholy
Behaviour Patterns:	Denial
Sound:	Weepy
Taste:	Spicy, pungent

Brief Summary: **Metal** is about breath and blockages, the entrances of fresh **Ki** into your body, via the **(Yin) Lung Meridian**, and the exits of stagnant **Ki** and waste matter, via the **(Yang) Large Intestine Meridian**. In short, they are your gatekeeper and your garbage disposal meridians. **Metal** reflects your ability to inhale **Ki** through your nose and skin, your entire being, and your ability to expel all waste matter, both physical and emotional, all stagnant forms of **Ki**. Your sniffles and blocked nose and breathing problems and constipation and skin problems all reflect **Metal** imbalances, as does an obsession with wearing or avoiding white. Remember that snively child at school who seemed to have endless colds and kept dropping handkerchiefs around the classroom? A sudden craving for a curry dinner or any other pungent or spicy foods, like mustard, also characterises **Metal**.

Many depressives experience a shutdown in **Metal**, shallow breathing, loss of feeling, turning inward, chronic or unexplained sadness month after month. Excessive mourning following the loss of a loved one will affect **Metal**.

Element:	Water
Colour:	Blue, Black
Climate:	Cold
Direction:	North
Meridians:	Bladder (**Yang**); Kidney (**Yin**)
Body Part:	Bones
Sense Organ:	Ears
Sense:	Hearing
Fluid:	Urine
Emotion:	Fear, Paranoia
Behaviour Patterns:	Trembling
Sound:	Groaning
Taste:	Salty

Brief Summary: **Water** is about processing and eliminating fluids via the function of the **(Yin) Kidney Meridian** and its **(Yang)** partner, the **Bladder Meridian**, and their associated organs. But the **Kidney Meridian** also guides those milestones of growth, maturity, and decline in your life, from puberty to menopause. **Water** also controls your scaffolding, your inner core and structure, your bones, in a literal and metaphoric sense, and your teeth. The **Bladder Meridian** by location, controls your spine, and your autonomic nervous system, so we might work on this meridian to calm you down. The **Kidney Meridian** also brings the blueprint of your ancestral energy to you.

Water is about your sense of balance, your ability to handle cold, your sudden or recurring ear or hearing problems, vertigo and an obsession with wearing black. Water imbalances are reflected in those dark rings under your eyes, and those moments when you are hit by an unexplained fear or paranoia. **Water** is also about those days when you crave salty chips or sushi or kippers!

While examining each of the above elements and their associated meridians by turn, remember we're dealing with a sequence of movements or cycles from one Element to the next. The meridians themselves don't just dangle like spaghetti in the body. Ki energy flows from one meridian into the next, causing them to vibrate at different frequencies. The body is just an orchestra of **Ki** humming to Yin and Yang harmonies.

Ki in Many Directions

Ki is your life force, your energy, your 'quick'. **Ki** makes the difference between you and a T-bone steak. Western languages don't have an easy, convenient translation of **Ki**. It's more than just energy. **Ki** is the basic currency of Oriental philosophy, movement, harmonisation, medicine. Illnesses and problems are studied in terms of **Ki** imbalances, according to a diagnosis of deficiencies and excesses. Treatment is a harmonising process, achieved in acupuncture by inserting needles in specific points. The process is achieved in Zen Shiatsu by a combination of stretching and subtle pressure on at least two of the twelve meridians and related points, according to diagnosis.

Ki (Qi or Chi in Chinese)
(Caligraphy © Dr He Yan Wu)

Those of us who grew up in the West have to learn about **Ki** and Yin and Yang concepts when we study Oriental Medicine. We acquire a reverence for them that often amuses our Asian colleagues. In the Far East, words like Yin and Yang and **Ki** are part of the daily idioms used – no big deal. As Dr Jamie Wu, one of my colleagues and friends at the Academy of Oriental Medicine, says, a child will even use words like Yin or Yang to describe a covered or an open ditch.

How's Your Ki?

In Japanese, the word **Ki** pops up in countless contexts. Listen carefully next time you go to a Japanese movie. Even variations in the weather are described in terms of **Ki**. Here are a few other examples:

How are you = *genki desuka*.
Stay healthy = *genki-de*.
I love you = *daisuki*.
Sickness = *byoki* (literally, 'ailing **Ki**')
Hot-tempered = *ki no hayai*
Be unwilling (to do) = *ki ga susumanai*
(to be) Anxious about = *ki ni naru*
(to be) Pleased with = *ki ni iru*

One of my former students, April Chang of Taiwan, said to me one day, 'I don't know why you make such a fuss about **Ki**, Pam. For us, it's just like soya sauce.'

It's worth reflecting on the historic subtleties of meaning associated with *xue*, the Chinese character for acupuncture point. In *Hara Diagnosis: Reflections on the Sea*, Matsumoto and Birch remind us that in classical texts, *xue* actually meant a grave, or a cave, before its more modern meaning of a pit or a hole. To help the journey of the soul, the location of gravesites was determined by pre-Han geomancers according to the arrangement of surrounding mountains and rivers, to ensure a harmonious relationship between heavenly and earthly energies. The art of geomancy is best known in the West today by its more popular term Feng Shui.

Traditional Chinese and Japanese Medicine share a similarly poetic view of the landscape of the body. Given the historic understanding of the character *xue*, an acupuncture (or pressure) point has more resonance and depth (literally) than in its inadequate Western translation 'point', as do the lyrical names of the points, such as *gushing spring* or *sun and moon*.

The Japanese term for a pressure point is *tsubo*. The actual character also implies depth, as in a ground floor and the basement below. But *tsubo* also means a vase in Japanese. During my early training in Zen Shiatsu, we were taught that the subtle, perpendicular application of **Ki** pressure on a *tsubo* resulted in depth and **Ki** expansion, like sinking into the bulbous base of a vase. With such imagery in mind, the concept of **Ki** transformation becomes three dimensional.

A basic training in Zen Shiatsu also emphasises **Ki** energy as being in a constant state of flux, in our bodies, and in our surroundings.

The use of translucent materials as in the shoji screens of traditional Japanese design convey subtle shifts in light and texture from dawn to dusk as a constant philosophical reminder of changing **Ki**. Quite a contrast to those countries with a tradition of using heavy curtains, where you don't know if it's 9.00 am or 9.00 pm.

The Japanese tradition of taking long, hot baths in bathrooms open to a beautiful garden emphasises a meditative awareness of changing **Ki** expressed through the seasonal shifts of the Five Elements. Cleansing and scrubbing is done *before* the deep bath, not during, enhancing the meditative qualities of the ritual. Westerners who build hot tubs in their gardens or on their back porches can enjoy similar experiences in a meditative spirit, if they use their tubs in all seasons. A dense urban setting (whether Tokyo, London, Berlin or New York) hardly offers the luxury of a garden bathroom unless you can afford a fancy penthouse. Most of us compromise by hanging graceful ferns in our tiny bathrooms.

Western architects who love designing entire houses with an indoor-outdoor-indoor appeal offer splendidly adventurous examples when designing their own homes. Swiss architect Andre Studer (a friend of the

<table>
<tr><td>June</td><td>May</td><td>April</td></tr>
</table>

June   May   April

December   November   October

'Flowers and Birds of the Twelve Months' by Yamamoto Soken (1683–1706), Edo Period, late seventeenth century (Asian Art Museum, San Francisco © The Avery Brundage Collection)

| March | February | January |

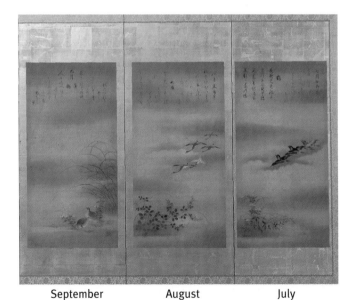

| September | August | July |

The pair of six folding screens (ink and colours on silk) shows a graceful shift of seasonal symbols and plants from month to month, from the plum blossom and bush-warbler for spring, to the bush-clover and wild goose for autumn. (Read from top right to left.)

late Frank Lloyd Wright) created a home near Zurich that feels like an enclosed garden. This is not just a matter of lots of plate glass and open space, sloping ceilings, skylights and natural wood. The house is actually landscaped *around* nature (rather than vice versa), with unusual dimensions and unconventional living spaces. Trees and beds of plants give you the feeling that you are living outside, or in a treehouse. Of course, you are protected from harsh winters by central heating, and a huge, traditional Swiss farmhouse oven. Studer designs according to harmonic principles, like a musician composing a piece of music. This is why his buildings are noted for their beautiful acoustics, like the Catholic church he designed in Kilchberg near the lake of Zurich.

Florentine architect Renato Severino designed his passive solar house overlooking Long Island Sound in Connecticut, USA with an lot of interior and exterior windows and skylights, and interior mirrored surfaces. The family could then enjoy the 'travels of the sun and moon', and where 'even a storm is beautiful', Severino told me when I wrote about him in my book *Decoration and Design for the 80s* some years ago in New York.

Seasonal symbols recur through many traditional Japanese art forms, of which the decorative folding screens of the Edo period from the seventeenth and eighteenth centuries are wonderful examples. Folding screens I saw in the permanent collection at San Francisco's Asian Art Museum offer the perfect format. The eye follows the graceful movement of one season into the next, through farming scenes, or through seasonal symbols such as the plum blossom and bush-warbler for spring, or the bush-clover and wild goose for autumn.

The early nineteenth century Zen Buddhist nun Rengetsu, accomplished in the martial arts as well as in pottery, verse and calligraphy, left us an exquisite legacy in a series of seasonal poems under the general title *Lotus Moon*.

In one poem, 'Gazing at the Moon Night after Night' she captures the Zen duality of movement-in-stillness-and-stillness-in-movement, or the duality of permanence and change, by honouring the autumn moon as a tie to a 'floating world'.

In the Inkling edition of *Lotus Moon*, translator John Stevens reminds us that the autumn moon is in itself a contemplative object for Buddhists, and a symbol of enlightenment.

In Japanese, even the days of the week reflect the Elements, the two exceptions being Monday (Moon) and Sunday (Sun). **Tuesday, Wednesday, Thursday, Friday, and Saturday**, are, respectively **Fire, Water, Wood, Metal, and Earth**.

The Six Elements (1928) by
René Magritte. **Fire** (flames),
Earth (torso), **Wood** (forest),
Water (window), **Air** (sky) and
Metal (bells). (Philadelphia
Museum of Art © Louise and
Walter Arensburg Collection)

Chapter 4

Experiencing The Five Elements

Teaching And Diagnosing

Some years ago I remember walking into a classroom where a colleague had just taught a class in the Five Elements. The diagram on the blackboard was chalked up in white and looked like a scrambled egg. If I couldn't figure out what was going on, how could the students? I stood there wondering how students had made sense of my own diagrams. I have used chalks in the Five Element colours ever since.

Similarly, and inspired by Elli Mann Langhof's Schule fur Shiatsu, Berlin, I ask all my students to come to class wearing the colour of the element to be studied. It's a lot of fun. And very instructive. Students are able to relate their own reactions to the colours in terms of likes and dislikes and insights into why they prefer one colour over another or why they avoid certain colours. We have noted the ways in which the colours, quite spontaneously, evoke moods, feelings and discussions associated with each element.

On **Wood Day** (Spring), students arrive looking fresh and crisp in varying shades of green: they're zippy and restless as they spread themselves around the room. When some choose olive green, others are quick to make jokes about the militaristic associations with the **Wood** element.

On **Fire Day** (Summer) they're ablaze in red and perspire easily: they're talkative and noisy, rushing to open windows and fan the air. They move away from one another to reduce some of the heat and intensity. If the group is large and there isn't enough space, students seem to bounce off one another. Arguments break out.

On **Earth Day** (Indian, or Late Summer), they're a harvest feast in shades of yellow, gold, brown and orange. The light seems to vibrate with their colours. They become nurturing, reflective, and more attentive to one another.

On **Metal Day** (Autumn) the students are stark in their white or grey attire, clinical and formal. They are subdued, distant. There's a melancholy sense of loss. They gaze wistfully out of the window at the bare branches. Winter is on its way. They feel chilly, run to fetch sweaters and turn up the heat.

On **Water Day** (Winter) they're sombre in black and dark blue, and huddle close together on the floor like a Greek Chorus. I ask myself, is this the same group that filled the room with their sparky energy on **Fire Day**? The room looks half empty. Some find the mood depressing, fearful. Some sink into dark moods. Memories surface from the depths. Everyone wants to go home early.

In Austin, one of my former students, Ginger Hunkin, noted a big difference when she first started driving a black car. 'Other drivers let me go ahead of them,' she says. When another former student, Eve Berens, drove to school in a red shirt on **Fire Day**, she said, 'No car wanted to argue with me'. She noted the reaction, because she never wears red and had to borrow a red shirt for class. (Interestingly, their experiences of red and black confirm the Royal Automobile Club survey about the colours that dominate the road – see Chapter 1, Touch, Taste and See the Five Elements.)

On each respective day of our Five Element weekend courses in Europe, we burn candles in the different colours, spread colourful cloths with CDs, art, books, poems, photos, foods, fruit, flowers, anything to express and experience the sensory and cultural aspect of each element. We listen to flamenco, tango and salsa music on **Fire Day**. Mozart's clarinet and oboe music on **Wood Day**. During one **Metal Day** while teaching in Berlin, I played CDs of classical Malian string instruments and songs of the Copperbelt miners of Zambia. On **Earth Day**, after my time in Costa Rica, I played cassettes of the rain forest. We listened to CDs of ocean sounds and the haunting calls of the whales on **Water Day**.

Teaching the subject in the mountains and woods of East Quebec province for Shiatsu-Ki Quebec school during the late 1980s and early 1990s was a gift. The subject came alive as we hiked, swam and gathered around huge campfires at night. On a midday stroll during a 1994 class in Berlin, we came across an AIDS prevention information poster showing a row of condoms in the colours of the Five Elements. We'll never forget that day.

I encourage my students to use pens or markers in Five Element colours in their textbooks, throughout their notes, diagrams and their diagnostic diagrams. Not only is this a marvellous training tool for the mind, but it also helps to sharpen their diagnostic skills and it makes learning a lot more fun. It encourages them to be acutely observant of the colours their patients wear, not just in terms of likes and dislikes, but the assorted choices for trousers, skirts, sweaters, coats and accessories. 'If they come to you for problems with poor circulation,' I tell them, 'note the colours they choose for their gloves, socks, and scarves, in particular. Discourage blue or black and encourage them to wear more red.' Also: 'If they have high blood pressure, discourage them from wearing too much red, and encourage them to wear more blue. If they have low blood pressure, discourage blue and encourage red. Watch their general preferences in colours and note any sudden changes. If someone never wears yellow and suddenly arrives dressed up in a canary yellow outfit, find out if they're having problems with digestion.'

It's equally useful to become aware of changes in facial hue according to the elements – an art, of course, when working within a variety of skin tones and ethnic backgrounds. Dr Jamie Wu, formerly professor and chief acupuncturist of Chengdu teaching hospital in China, talks about the challenge presented by fifty-six different ethnic groups in China!

Generally speaking, dark black rings under the eyes can reflect kidney (**Water**) deficiencies, burn-out, lack of sleep, and an inability to replenish the Yin of the constitution through sleep, rest. Dr Wu also advises students to be aware of a yellowish-green tint for jaundice, or other liver problems; excessive red for heart problems (and to be aware of a possible emergency if the red hue changes to a black hue, because '**Water** is dominating **Fire**'). In Western medicine, the equivalent would probably be blue lips.

If coughing produces mucus with a salty taste, the kidneys (**Water**) could be the source: if mucus tastes acidy, check the liver (**Wood**). A bitter taste on the tip of the tongue (**Fire**) can imply a lack of sleep. A very pale, white skin can imply respiratory problems, and in some cases, chronic constipation. Hamburg-based Dr Wilfried Rappenecker – who combines his training in Western medicine with his acupuncture and shiatsu practice and teaching – told me about one of his patients, who always wore white, and had a very white skin. The man was chronically constipated. Interestingly, some family problems were discovered to be a source of these tightly overcontrolled patterns, as they eased after an intense Christmas with his parents.

Tips for Diagnosis

My colleague Matthias Wieck has developed a unique Five Element diagnostic tool in his shiatsu and acupuncture practice in Berlin. He places a stack of sheets in the Five Element colours on the floor, and asks his patients to choose a colour for the mat. Over the years, he has noted that patients suffering consistently from backpain, choose blue sheets (**Water** Element is frequently associated with back problems). Sceptical, I agreed to experiment with his theory one day in Berlin. Out of six patients, no less than five of them selected colours related to their problems:

- Circulatory   –   Pink (**Fire**)
- Back   –   Blue (**Water**)
- Digestion   –   Yellow (**Earth**)
- Painful tendons and joints –   Green (**Wood**)
- Asthma   –   White (**Metal**)

Fascinated, I decided to expand on the experiment when I returned to the USA. I gave patients a box of coloured pencils and asked them to choose any colours at random to shade or 'x' areas of their chronic or acute pain on charts of body outlines. Generally, I have found patients will use red for acute and blue for chronic pain. But beyond this, they often choose colours that match their problem meridians (even when they don't consciously know the connection), like green for shoulder problems and yellow for digestion.

I also nailed a meridian chart to a corkboard, and scattered different coloured pins underneath. I asked my patients to track or cluster the pins on the chart to show me where they experienced acute or chronic pain. This helped patients externalise their pain and areas of tension in a way they found very illuminating. In addition, their choice of pin colour on specific pressure points and meridians offered me clues as to the source and condition of their problems, according to the Five Elements.

I remember one patient with rheumatoid arthritis, who came to me regularly for six months. One day, she stuck green pins (**Wood**) on the chart on the joints that caused her the most pain. So we talked about issues of unresolved anger. She agreed wholeheartedly that she still felt very angry with some former business colleagues who, it was clear to me, had treated her appallingly. 'But you are allowing these people to sit in your joints,' I said, and she agreed. I then taught her some **Ki** exercises for moving stagnant energy out of the joints, exercises that were fluid, visual and easy for her to do at home. She found these highly beneficial, especially as they were painless and required very little movement.

Another patient became very reflective one afternoon after she inserted blue pins (**Water**) on the chart to highlight the areas of her lower back pain. She said, 'I don't know if there's a connection, but I've just remembered a recurring dream I had as a child. In my dream, my brother kept stabbing me in the kidneys. I was terrified of him as a child, but grew out of it. No big deal. But now I think I understand why I don't seem to have had a connection with my lower back until now.'

How Do We Perceive Colours?

Physicists, philosophers and artists all contribute to our understanding of how colours work, how we perceive them, and how we react to them emotionally.

During the late seventeenth century, Sir Isaac Newton directed a beam of sunlight through a prism. The beam fanned out into a beautiful spectrum of colours. He then directed the spectrum through a second prism – and achieved light. Newton believed that light travels in straight lines; other physicists analysed light as different wavelengths. Einstein reconciled both views by describing light as bundles of energy, or 'photons', capable of moving in lines – and in wavelengths. Newton also related different colours to notes on the diatonic scale:

> F = Green; C = Red; G = Blue; D = Orange;
> A = Indigo; E = Yellow; B = Violet.

Goethe, as scientist, poet and author, threw purist physicists into a tizzy by declaring in his famous *Farbenlehre*, that 'optical illusion is optical truth'. As Erlangen-Nurnbeg University professor of maths, Dr Hubert Berens, told me, 'Goethe was looking at the *Farbenlehre* not from a physical point of view, but more from a physiological viewpoint.' Modern physicist/philosophers like Carl van Weizsacker, former director of the Max Planck Institute of Physics and Philosophy, of Göttingen, are now recognising the value of Goethe's contribution.

Goethe's observations about shadows and afterimages, and the effects of one colour bouncing off another, would probably have made him feel more at home in an artist's studio than in the physics lab of his time. When we stand in front of a favourite painting, we respond spontaneously, and that's Goethe's point. Our response to the mind-teasing surrealism of Dali, or to the gaudy, sensual Gauguin view of Tahiti women and flowers, may be very different from our response to the softly subtle views of Monet's haystacks. But unless we are doing a technical study, we wouldn't initially stand there and imagine the artist experimenting with assorted colour combinations, dyes and textures, to achieve the whole.

Imagine a World without Colours!

We take colours very much for granted. They're part of our landscape – art, graphics, colour Xerox, colour TVs and Windows '98. How easy it is to forget that the great Italian Renaissance figures of da Vinci and Michaelangelo struggled to raise the status of painters to the status of mathematician and architect. After all, those painters were considered scruffy artisans who hung about with dirty hands and spattered clothes!

85

As Anthea Cullen reminds us in *Techniques of the Impressionists*, colour was considered vulgar. Colour meant nature and the raw senses. We have the Impressionists to thank for exploding this classical view by experimenting with an array of bright and pastel colours and techniques.

Colour perception bounces back and forth between artist and external world, artist and canvas, canvas and viewer, in very individual ways. Similarly, visually challenged people develop unique relationships with colour that can teach something to those of us who take our perceptions of colour very much for granted. Frances Futterman facilitates the Achromatopsia Network in Berkeley, California, on behalf of those like herself, who have no colour vision at all. She has developed extraordinary abilities to teach and rehabilitate visually challenged people through her own experiences and scientific documentation (described in Dr Oliver Sacks' *The Island of the Colourblind*). Ms Futterman told me in a telephone interview from her home in Berkeley California that her sense of smell and taste are intense, adding, 'I'm a good cook and a fussy eater!'

Ms Futterman is quick to emphasise the difference between her congenital (retinal) achromatopsia and acquired (cerebral) achromatopsia, such as that suffered by the painter described by Dr Sacks in *Anthropologist on Mars*. Retinal achromatopsia is due to the non-functioning of those photoreceptors (cones) in the retina we need for three things: colour vision, daytime vision and fine detail vision. Cerebral achromatopsia is caused by damage to the brain.

Because of his prior memory of colour, the colourblind painter described his world in terms of varying shades of black, grey and white. By contrast Ms Futterman, like other congenital achromats, cannot 'see' colours, but adds 'Being colour-blind is the least of our problems.' She emphasises their extreme sensitivity to light, especially during the daytime, and with dramatic changes in vision from place to place. Night vision is more comfortable, more acute.

Therapies like bio-energetics bring 'energy' to her eyes and a heightened sensitivity to the vibration of colours, especially red, orange, or yellow. In workshops where participants would be asked to concentrate or meditate on a colour, Futterman could choose familiar objects, such as blood for red and butter for yellow.

I know of another achromat who responds strongly to glasses with red lenses. Even though she cannot 'see' red, the effect of the colour unsettles her, disturbs her nervous system. This means red has an intense frequency.

Colours in Action

Depending on your bias – physicist or artist, or both, you can develop a whole new understanding of how you relate to Five Element colours in terms of how they bounce off you emotionally. Or, how they affect your health or mood when they share your home or office with you. For a quick impression, study Rene Magritte's polyptych *The Six Elements 1921*, from the Philadelphia Museum of Art. The panels show **Fire** (Flames), **Earth** (a woman's torso), **Wood** (a vivid green forest), **Water** (Windows), **Air** (blue sky), and **Metal** (sleigh bells) (see page 78).

As California surgeon Leonard Shlain reminds us in his book *Art and Physics, Parallel Visions in Space, Time and Light*, 'Colour precedes words and antedates civilisation, connected as it is to the subterranean ground-waters of the archaic limbic system.' Or, in more everyday terms, a baby responds to bright colours before it learns words.

Red (**Fire**) heats, and blue (**Water**) cools, whether in science or art, Western or Oriental Medicine, language, or decor. When excessive, our **Fire** and **Water** can lapse into bipolar disorders. They are our south to north and our Yang to Yin extremes. We have to watch them carefully to make sure they don't throw the others out of balance. The Russians have a wonderful expression for this: 'Fire and Water are good servants but bad masters' (*Ogon I voda-horoshie sloogie, no plohie hozyaeva*).

Mix red light (**Fire**), green light (**Wood**) and blue light (**Water**), to produce white light (**Metal**). Mix them in varying proportions to produce all the other colours. Green (**Wood**) and red (**Fire**) mix to produce yellow (**Earth**). Historically, the blunt colours of the Elements just matched the surrounding landscape. **Earth** is yellow in the region of China where the Five Elements were described. But as any world traveller knows, **Earth** comes in countless variations of brown, red, yellow, ochre and limestone, and a multilayered combination, as in America's vivid southwest captured by many of Georgia O'Keeffe's dramatic paintings.

Today, in spite of hundreds of colour variations available to us in paints, dyes, objects and textures, designers like New York's Sophie Keir claim that people in dense urban settings long to return to a few, simple landscape colours in their homes. These are based on nature's own dyes of mustard, cornflower blue, indigo, lavender, beet and sage.

You and Your Five Element Colours

At this stage you are probably itching to see how you match the Elements. Go to your clothes closet and organise every item according to blocks of colour: green, red, pink, yellow (and gold, orange, brown and khaki), white, silver and grey, blue and black. Take a step back and look at the palette of your clothes, your shirts, blouses, T-shirts, pants, skirts, sweaters, socks and underwear.

- Are the colours fairly evenly distributed?
- Or do you have masses of white clothes, and very little yellow, brown, orange, khaki, or gold?
- Do you have enough black clothes to supply your local undertaker?
- Or enough red clothes for your fire station? Do you have very little red, but an excess of pink? Or vice versa?
- Is your closet dominated by different shades of green?
- Now, make a note of the distribution of colours according to inner and outer garments, casual and sports clothes, business and formal wear.
- Do you have an abundance of one colour and very little of another?

Of course, your clothes will also reflect your preferences according to the colour and tone of your skin, hair and eyes, so balance your diagnosis with this knowledge.

As my black hair turned increasingly grey during my thirties, I began to prefer purple over brown. I enjoy wearing pastel colours and white when I am tanned, but feel washed out if I wear them in winter. Today, I notice

A popular Russian expression advises: 'Fire and water make good servants but bad masters'.

that my closet is dominated by reds and purples, followed by blue and black, followed by white. There is very little green. **Earth** tones are lacking in my closet, because they make me look like a corpse. But they dominate my home. My past homes in London, my homes in New York and Texas include brown and rust textiles and natural wood and oatmeal or rich dark brown floors or carpeting.

Years ago in London during my days in full-time journalism, but during a break-up in my personal life, I happened to buy a hand-woven Greek blanket in orange, cream and brown, but knew nothing then about the Law of the Five Elements. Only now, on looking back, do I realise that I instinctively sought **Earth** colours to balance and 'root' my fragile emotional state.

A swift analysis of my closet follows. I am a Sagittarian, so there is a lot of **Fire** in me and I have no problem expressing it. I come from a family of chronic migraine sufferers, and yes, I notice how little green there is in my closet, and contemplate the problems I have making decisions and expressing anger. Oh yes – anger and power are tough issues for those of us women from northern European backgrounds, as we were raised with the idea that they are somehow 'unladylike', and society shuns strong woman.

I notice that when I wear green (seldom), how sparky and energetic and invigorated I feel (a mental note to myself, wear green more often). I have noticed, however, that when I obsess about pink, or make an impulse buy of a pink shirt or blouse, I invariably come down with a migraine. A block is building up in my circulation. And my obsession with pink is a warning bell. Clearly, a very different migraine is en route from those (**Wood** migraines) prompted by flashing light bulbs or zigzaggy polka-dot patterns, or **Metal** migraines prompted by dry, stale air.

While discussing Five Element colours with my German editor Susanne Warmuth, she suddenly remembered that a friend of hers wore yellow obsessively, and that the woman had always wanted to be an opera singer. 'Don't you see the connection?' I remarked. 'The **Earth** element is not only associated with the colour yellow, but with singing and a singsong voice!'

Years ago I had an interesting experiencing involving the colour white (**Metal**). In my first years as a shiatsu instructor, I was required to wear white *gi*, (like the martial artists) at the Shiatsu Education Centre (now the Ohashi Institute) in New York City. I remember one bitterly cold week when I travelled to Montreal to teach, and developed bronchitis. I spent the days in bed and coughed and spluttered my way through my evening classes. I broke the school's strict regulation *gi* code because it was suddenly impossible for me to wear white. I couldn't even bear to see it hanging in my hotel closet. So, I packed my white *gi* out of sight. I wanted the warmth and comfort of a cosy red sweatsuit, and told my students why. Dr Lise Ste-Marie, a physician who was one of my students at that time and has since become a dear friend, remarked during the class that she suddenly realised all her asthmatic patients wore white to excess.

So there we had a crisp example of two aspects of the **Metal** element: my aversion to white while experiencing acute bronchitis, and her chronic asthmatic patients' obsession with white.

During the years when I had my practice at Dr Linda Li's chiropractic clinic in New York, a patient walked in one day wearing an assortment of shades of green, from her beret down to her socks and shoes. **Wood** loomed at me. I had never seen her dress like this before.

My immediate question was, 'What biting decision are you trying to make in your life?' She looked startled, 'How did you know?'

She admitted she was in an obsessive bind, unable to decide between continuing her therapy practice in the city or moving it to the country.

In the past, red (**Fire**) was considered divine and sacred in some cultures (Egyptian) and healing in others (medieval doctors in Britain used to wear red coats), according to Faber Birren, author of the classic *Colour Psychology and Colour Therapy*. Birren also writes about the medieval Arab physician Avicenna, who advised anyone with a nosebleed to avoid staring at brilliant red, but believed in the healing powers of red flowers for blood disorders. In other medical studies, red has been known to cause an increase in blood pressure, while blue causes blood pressure to drop.

Your Colour Palette and Your Health

Let's take an even closer look at your own personal palette. You know which colours make you feel wonderful and which colours drain you. You like some colours in the summer and different colours in the winter, perhaps?

You have various ways of assessing your colour diagnosis. Firstly, look at your general pattern, and note the colours you wear to excess and the colours you avoid. Secondly, think about a recent or past pattern involving a colour choice, or an obsession or aversion, especially if these reflect specific events in your life, such as changes (relating to home, partner, job, country, town, etc.) recent illnesses, a loss, or recent joys.

Remember that an avoidance of one colour or an obsession with another colour can both reflect imbalances in their related organs and meridian systems. Jot down all your observations. Let's see how they match the other characteristics of each element, namely, the associated organs, systems, problems, emotions, tastes and so on. This will help you expand your initial connections.

Choose pencils in the relevant Five Element colours and highlight those words and categories that currently mirror you. Draw a square box in those same colours around words and categories that reflect you in the past. Here goes:

Are You a Wood Type?

Spring, Green, Wind, The East, Anger, Shouting, Decision, Indecision

Gall Bladder: Has it been removed? Do you suffer from gallstones? Have you ever taken the Pill? Do you have cholesterol problems? Do you suffer from anger turned inward? Do you have problems digesting fatty foods?

Liver: Have you experienced Hepatitis A, B, C, D or E? Do you have problems with metabolism (processing fats, proteins, or carbohydrates)? Do you have an iron/vitamin A deficiency? Do you have blood disorders? Do you experience outbursts of anger? Do you have prostate or testicular problems?

General Problems: Do you experience any of the following: tight muscles, brittle nails, tension, indecision, eye strain, poor eyesight, tears (dry eyes or weepy eyes, especially on windy days)? Do you cry easily? Or rarely? Do you shout a lot? Do you have migraines/headaches on the left or the right or both sides of your head? Are the headaches triggered by eyestrain, or flashing light bulbs, by zigzag patterns, or by too much computer work or TV? Are they triggered by foods or other allergies? By stress? Are they triggered by: changes in temperature, or air pressure, or by any other changes in the weather, or east or south-easterly winds? Generally, are you bothered by the spring or windy days? Do you suffer from allergies in the springtime? Do you like/crave/avoid sour foods and drinks (lemon, lime, sour pickles, sauerkraut, sour plums, sour apples, rose hips)?

If necessary, elaborate on any items you have encircled.

Are You a Fire Type?

Summer, Red, Pink, Heat, The South, Joy, Laughter

Heart: Do you suffer from angina? Have you ever had heart surgery? Have you ever had a heart transplant? Or a Triple Bypass? Have you ever experienced arrhythmia? Or any other heart problems? Are you an artist and have you ever experienced a creative block?

Small Intestine: Have you ever experienced an Ileus (intestinal block?) Do you have problems absorbing and processing your food – do you notice bits of undigested food in your stool? Do you eat too quickly? Are you studying for exams at the moment and finding it difficult to absorb facts? Do you ever have severe menstrual cramps?

Triple Heater: (This is the meridian which controls your body's thermostat and lymph system). Do you travel a lot? Do you suffer from jetlag? Do you suffer when the temperature changes suddenly? Do you have problems adapting to change (home, job, environment, country, time zone, partner, etc.)? Do you have any problems with your immune system? Are you menopausal and experiencing hot flushes?

Heart Constrictor (Pericardium): Do you have any problems with your circulation? Do you have cold hands and cold feet, for example? Or do you have sweaty hands and sweaty feet? Are you suffering from insomnia? Are you experiencing vivid dreams at the moment? Do you have varicose veins? Are you going through a divorce or separation? Are you going through the menopause?

General Problems: Do you have any speech difficulties? Do you get tongue-tied sometimes? Or are you ever over-talkative? Is your tongue sensitive to certain foods? Do you laugh when you're nervous? Do you giggle a lot? Do you perspire a lot, or not enough? Does summer or extreme heat bother you? Do you like/crave/avoid bitter foods or drink (dark chocolate, coffee, tea, cocoa, dandelion, burdock, spinach, camomile, alfalfa, radish, rye, angostura)?

If necessary, elaborate on any items you have encircled.

Are You an Earth Type?

Late Summer (Indian Summer), Brown, Orange, Gold, Yellow, Khaki, The Centre, Dampness, Worry, Singing

Stomach: Do you experience any acidity? Or bloating after eating? Or burping? Are you suffering from ulcers? Have you experienced any eating disorders (past or present)? Do you have any problems with your parents? Do you have any problems swallowing? Do you have any menstrual problems? Or any problems with your uterus? Do you have any breast problems? Are you having any problems with lactation?

Spleen/Pancreas: Do you have any menstrual problems? Do you have problems with your ovaries, or with ovulation? Do you suffer from PMS? Do you have problems with fertility? Do you have any digestive problems? Do you suffer from sugar highs or lows? Are you a diabetic? Do you have knee problems? Do you have memory problems?

General Problems: Do you ever feel ungrounded? Do you ever worry obsessively? Do you hear yourself speaking in a sing-song voice when you are stressed? Do you ever over-salivate? Or do you suffer from a dry mouth? Do you have cracks or pimples at the corners of your mouth? Are you bothered by the late summer (Indian Summer)? Does dampness or damp weather depress or bother you generally? Are you allergic to mould? Are you experiencing a difficult menopause? Do you like, crave, avoid sweet foods and drinks (candy, desserts, honey, maple syrup, beets, most fruits, sweet potato, sweet liqueurs)?

If necessary, elaborate on any items you have encircled.

Are You a Metal Type?

Autumn, White, Grey, the West, Dryness, Melancholy, Weeping

Lung: Do you ever experience any breathing difficulties? Do you have asthma, or allergies? Do you have bronchitis? Is your breathing very shallow? Do you smoke? Does your work involve inhaling toxic substances?

Large Intestine: Do you suffer from chronic constipation? Do you feel stuck somewhere in your life? Do you suffer from diarrhoea? Do you suffer from irritable bowel syndrome? Do you suffer from gas? Or from bloating?

General Problems: Are your allergies seasonal, or general? Do you suffer from seasonal or general skin problems? Do you have a very pale skin? Do you experience itchiness? Do you suffer from a dry nose, or from too much mucus? Do you feel sad for no reason? Do you ever feel so depressed you lose a sense of your body and each move is an effort? Are you obsessed about wearing white, or do you avoid white altogether? Does the late autumn (dry, hard ground, stark white sky, bare trees) bother or sadden you at all? Do you have a keen/or a poor sense of smell? Do you like/crave/avoid spicy (pungent) foods and drinks (curry, bloody mary, chillies, garlic, onion, ginger, horseradish, cinnamon, cloves, cayenne)?

If necessary, elaborate on any items you have encircled.

Are You a Water Type?

Winter, Black, Dark Blue, The North, The Cold, Paranoia, Fear, Groaning

Bladder: Do you suffer from back problems (chronic or acute, upper or lower back)? Do you have neck problems? Do you experience a lot of central headaches (especially migraines)? Do you have cystitis, or do you suffer from chronic bladder problems or bladder infections?

Kidney: Do you tire easily? Do you often experience burn-out? Do you have chronic lower back pain? Have you ever experienced a kidney disease? Are you on dialysis? Have you just experienced a trauma or shock? Has someone dear to you died recently? Do you suffer from memory problems? Do you have menstrual problems? Do you suffer from a loss of hair (through chemotherapy or other reasons)?

General Problems: Do your bones ache when you are cold? Do you suffer from osteoporosis? Do you suffer from hearing problems? Are you experiencing earache, or a constant buzz or ringing in your ears? Do you have problems with equilibrium? Do you moan and groan a lot? Do you suffer from incontinence? Does the winter, or extreme cold bother you? Do you like/crave/avoid salty foods and drink (salted fish, kippers, roll mop herrings, sushi, miso, salty chips and peanuts, salty lassi, salted crackers)?

If necessary, elaborate on any items you have encircled.

What Are Your Best Hours?

Each organ and system in your body has a **peak functioning time**, a two-hour bite every twenty-four hours, and a **low time** in the matching two-hour bite twelve hours later. For example, I am very much a morning person, and was born at 9.40am Central Time in San Francisco del Oro, Chihuahua, Mexico. But between 9.30pm – 10.00pm I nod off to sleep, regardless of where I am in the world, and what I am doing. Friends have even photographed me going to sleep at 10.00pm at dinner parties in London or New York.

- Would you describe yourself as a morning person?
- An afternoon person? Or an evening person?
- Or a night owl?
- At what time were you born?
- Generally speaking, do you feel energetic around the same time as your birth time each day or night? Or do you feel sleepy around that time?

Here's how the organs match the time bites.

- Circle the time zones matching your energy peaks
- Square the time zones matching your lowest ebb

Metal

3.00–5.00am (**Lungs**): Best time for meditation, as practised by a number of religious orders. Benedictines and Zen Buddhists rise before 5.00am for this purpose.

5.00–7.00am (**Large Intestine**): Best time for a bowel movement. Big elimination time. Also the time when the sperm count is highest!

Earth

7.00–9.00am (**Stomach**): Best time for breakfast.

9.00–11.00am (**Spleen**): Best time to digest breakfast.

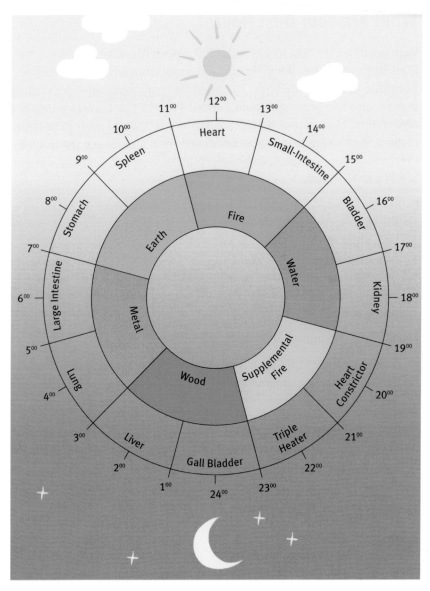

The Chinese Clock. What are your best or worst hours? The twenty-four hour clock shows the 'peak functioning time' of the meridians and their related organs and systems, in sequence. The relative 'low time' is twelve hours after the 'peak time'. Relate your birth times, your highs and lows, to this clock.

98

Absolute Fire

11.00–13.00pm (**Heart**): Now you know why heart patients are told to relax around noon. Remember Noel Coward's witty song: 'Mad Dogs and Englishmen go out in the Midday Sun'?

13.00–15.00pm (**Small Intestine**): Best time for lunch and siesta.

Water

15.00–17.00pm (**Bladder**): Good time to process and review the day. Get up from your desk and stretch your back. Good time for meetings if you haven't had a liquid lunch!

17.00–19.00pm (**Kidney**): Time to slow down, relax. Many people experience weariness around 18.00pm. Popular sundowner time in hot climates. A good time to eat your evening meal.

Supplemental Fire

19.00–21.00pm (**Heart Constrictor**, also known as **Pericardium**): Probably the time when most people eat their evening meal, preferably earlier than later. Good time for those romantic candlelight suppers, because it's also a fine time for lovemaking!

21.00–23.00pm (**Triple Heater**): Also supposed to be a good lovemaking time. Basically a time when you need cosy warmth and protection from the night.

Wood

23.00–1.00am (**Gall Bladder**): People who eat late often experience migraines at this time. If you wake up within this time, your mind could be spinning around some decision. Don't lie in bed and fret. Get up and do something, This can help to straighten out your decisions.

1.00–3.00am (**Liver**): Similarly, if you wake up during these hours, your mind is probably over-actively planning something. Get up and work or read. Often this helps to resolve and calm the mind.

List all the items you circled alongside the appropriate element.

Does one element outweigh the next? Are you a **Wood** or a **Water** person? Are there any elements that do not mirror you at all? Do you see any connecting patterns? Where do you fit in? This might be a good time for reflection. Are you surprised by what you have discovered? Have you learnt something new about yourself? Are you able to connect some of the loose ends in your life? Don't be too alarmed about an occasional problem – concentrate on those that repeat themselves or create a pattern in the element cycles. One of my former students, Randy Sexton, who specialises in psychiatric nursing, told me about a patient who experienced fear attacks every day between 3.00pm and 5.00pm (**Water/bladder time**/associated with fear and trauma).

Colour Meditations

If a lot of thoughts are running around in your mind right now, there is a very simple way of anchoring them, just by contemplating the colours of the elements.

Find a quiet spot and sit comfortably for a few moments. Close your eyes and breathe deeply. Imagine yourself in a green room. Enjoy the freshness of the colour. Sit in your green room as long as you like and watch your reactions; be conscious of the particular shade of green in your vision. As soon as you feel ready, move your mind into a red room, bold and dramatic. Again, observe your reaction, the effect on your breathing, your thoughts. Move into a pink room and observe the change and effect on you.

Take your time, don't rush, but don't force yourself to stay in one room longer than you need to. Move on to a yellow room, bright, cheery, and observe the change from the feelings you had in the previous rooms. Stay in your yellow room as long as you like. Then move into a clean, sharp white room. Observe the shift in pace in your thoughts and breathing, or any other physical reaction to the different rooms. Again, and in your own time, move to a blue room, any shade of blue that comes through spontaneously, and remain there until you feel ready to close the meditation.   ⟶

Don't open your eyes just yet. Sit and contemplate all the rooms for a moment and try to remember those that felt most welcoming and comfortable, and those you wanted to hurry through, and why. Did any of the rooms remind you of a particular room in your home, or elsewhere, or a favourite restaurant or shop?

This meditation can help you focus on the colours that soothe, calm and restore you, and the colours that agitate or unsettle you. Contrast the way you feel about colours today compared with the way you felt during your adolescence. Or did any of your favourite colours change after you went through a divorce or some other trauma?

Use this meditation creatively in any way you choose, for more insight into your relationship with each of the Five Elements, for guidance on the decor you are considering for your new home, or just to enhance a few peaceful moments for yourself in the morning or evening.

Chapter 5

Your Home and the Five Elements

◀ Choose your fruits and veggies
according to Five Element colours,
like this display outside a shop in
Fontvieille, Provence, France.
(Photo © Nancy Scanlan)

Feng Shui

Feng Shui – the art of creating harmonious living and work environments according to **Ki** principles of balancing Yin and Yang – is becoming increasingly popular in homes and offices on both sides of the Atlantic. Five Element solutions are part of Feng Shui, which actually means 'the way of wind and water'. Feng = **Wind** and Shui = **Water**.

There are many different approaches to Feng Shui. But there are also many so-called 'experts' with nothing more than a weekend of training. So – be careful. Research the subject well before seeking professional consultants – and check their credentials. Be wary of 'experts' who charge hundreds of pounds and advise you to make hugely impractical and costly changes to your space. Be wary of outrageous advice. One Feng Shui consultant had the nerve to tell an architect friend of mine in Germany that her marriage failed because her kitchen was in the wrong place, prompting her husband (also an architect) to eat his meals away from home!

In her work *Feng Shui for the Home*, British architect Evelyn Lip tells the story of the businessman who sought promotion, so was advised by his Feng Shui consultant to drive up steps every evening. He never got promoted, but he spent a fortune replacing his damaged tyres! Be guided by common sense, not nonsense. Start working out the raw basics for yourself.

When I worked as a journalist in London several years ago, before Feng Shui was popular in the West, I remember a top design consultant complaining about a new client. 'He wants us to re-design his offices and logo to boost business,' said the designer. 'But during our site visit we discovered factory workers had to use the most disgusting, freezing cold toilets. We told him this had to be the first priority. A cosmetic design overhaul was pointless.' So, Feng Shui is also about ethics, although we do hear horror stories of its misuse for purposes of profit and exploitation.

In Five Element terms, be guided by advice that is appropriate and practical for your particular region, country, geography and climate. What may be appropriate for Shanghai, Hong Kong, Tokyo, Kyoto or Singapore may not be appropriate for you in Berlin, London, Zurich,

Dublin or New York. And remember, Feng Shui is about good circulation of **Ki** in your home or office, in the same way that good health mirrors a good circulation of **Ki** in your body.

New York-born Anne Gray, a former cancer researcher and radiation therapist now specialising in Oriental Medicine, told me she trained in Feng Shui after working in hospice care with the terminally ill. 'Some people returned home and recovered. Others with the same prognosis went home and deteriorated rapidly,' she observed. This made her realise that the home environment had to be one of several contributing factors. Creating a healing environment is the inspiration behind Gray's Feng Shui consultancy in Austin, Texas. She follows the Pyramid School of Feng Shui, created in the USA by Nancilee Wydra with a contemporary, Western approach. Gray offers some simple guidelines: space should be safe, functional, comfy and clean. Clutter creates bad Feng Shui.

The Five Elements add another dimension, or solution, to problem areas. 'Apply the Five Elements to your home in the same way you would apply them to a patient,' she says.

Rooms and Colours

Begin with the obvious. Examine your house or flat in terms of compass, climate and colour. If a room is cold, apply warm (**Fire**) colours. If it is hot, apply cool (**Water** or **Metal**) colours. Similarly, don't use a lot of red in the room of a hyperactive child – choose cool blue colours, or a deeply calming forest green. Nurturing **Earth** colours (yellow, terracotta, khaki, brown) are good for a dining room, and for the bedroom of a family member who is somewhat insecure and needs reassurance and grounding.

If you want to spice up your bedroom, add some hot sexy reds. Red walls (especially in a small room) might be overwhelming, but you could experiment with a dash here and there, like cosy red flannel sheets in the winter, or a painting with a strong red image, or a large bowl of brilliant red flowers. Pink is safe, and a symbol of lasting relationships. Avoid a peachy pink – it's good for a hotel bedroom and a quick weekend fling, but not for a permanent relationship! Bubblegum pink is said to have a calming effect on a roomful of young delinquents.

I once had an interesting chat with some psychiatric nurses, who were also students of mine, in Zurich, about the effects of decor on mental patients. 'Red makes them aggressive,' I was told, 'but light green is very calming.' Similarly, industrial designers have discovered that a soft, light green is appropriate for factories and mills. This is probably because it is gentle on the eyes of people involved in detailed work. Similarly, green is a traditional choice for libraries.

Fresh green colours (**Wood**), are generally good for creativity and inspiration, which is why it didn't surprise me to discover that green was Goethe's choice for his study in Frankfurt. As there are so many different shades of green, make your choice carefully, according to the balance of light in your workspace. If you don't want green walls, dot plants around your shelves and desk and window ledges, or dangle them from the ceiling. Avoid yellowish green walls, because this could make you feel liverish. According to Gray, green should also be avoided in cancer wards, because it promotes growth! Sage green, a lovely greyish green, is currently very popular, and a good mediator between **Metal** and **Wood** in the Five Elements.

I thought about some of my favourite restaurants around the world and realised there were several **Earthy** common denominators (apart from good wholesome food) that created an appealing ambience. These included yellow walls in shades lingering between egg yoke and buttercup, plenty of dark stained wood, terracotta and fresh flowers. So, play around with the concepts if you need to spruce up your dining room.

Metal as stark white gives a room a clean, airy effect – or a clinical effect – again, determined by climate and choice. In a cold climate, the extensive use of white is dauntingly stark unless well balanced with warm textures, colours, furniture and tall indoor plants. Cities that have extremely hot summers and bitingly cold winters, such as New York, require something of a balancing act. In my tiny New York upper west side apartment, my white walls were lovely in summer when the place was flooded with light, but felt very bleak in the lengthening shadows of autumn and winter. So I compromised by painting the walls a subtle, linen white (cream colour = **Earth**), that felt good in all seasons, and appropriately too, as **Earth** is the central, balancing element.

The selection of warm colours for a bathroom (a **Water** zone) certainly helps in a cold climate. In Britain, where bathrooms and toilets can be notoriously cold, avoid green, white, or pale blue. Choose peach or pink or a cosy wallpaper. Avoid (**Fire**) red because it's not wise to confine two extremes within a tight space. Imagine the density of steam if you took a hot shower surrounded by fire engine red walls. You'd think you'd died and gone to hell.

Tips

Five Element shapes are also worth remembering when you choose patterns, wallpaper, artwork, sculpture, furniture and motifs. **Fire** has an upward movement – like flames, or a steeple or spire, or even a simple triangle. Think about this in your choice of artwork, or select scenes of mountain landscapes (which gives you your triangle shape and connection to the external world), if you need a dash of **Fire** in a room but don't relish the idea of a red wall. **Wood**'s shape is rectangular. **Metal** is round. **Earth** is square. **Water** is reflected by wavy lines, by glass, and by windows.

Light and Dark

In places such as Texas, where the summers are long and hot, don't have a front door or glass-fronted porch facing west. In those Texan cities with relatively cold winters, avoid sliding glass doors on the north facing side of the house, for a very practical reason. Icy climatic conditions come blasting down from the north.

By contrast, in cold, northern climates, maximise a west and southern exposure. If your view is awful or faces a brick wall, but the light is good, insert a stained glass window or hang up panels of colourful stained glass to bring all Five Elements into the space.

Having lived in both the warm south and in the cold north, I am acutely aware of north/south differences in priorities. Many northerners have an obsession with good light and windows that attract it. This applies to those corner houses in Berlin or Zurich with windows on three sides to maximise exposure to views and good light. This would be unthinkable in a severely hot southern climate, because of the intensity and glare. People who have lived most of their lives in the hot south seem to prefer darker, cooler rooms or even heavily shaded homes. As I have spent most of my adult years in northern cities (London, New York, Berlin and Zurich), I find dark rooms depressing in any climate. Each room in my Austin, Texas home is light and airy, painted the same cream colour as my New York apartment, and with a similarly balancing effect. Blinds subdue glare when necessary.

I like the advice given by the famous American architect, the late Frank Lloyd Wright, who said there should be clear sight lines through a house, from the front door or windows through to the back garden, which is another reason why I chose my current home. While safety (visibility) is an obvious factor here, some Feng Shui experts have reservations about a clear, straight passageway between front and back door. They advise people to hang wind chimes in the space, or place a potted plant there. The art is to slow down the **Ki**, encourage it to meander and prevent it bolting through from front to back door like a freight train.

Keep Ki Flowing!

Good **Ki** moves in wavy lines, like water, so keep this in mind when you plan and place furniture in your home, or when you re-organise a room to maximise the use of space and flow. Watch the way friends and family move in and out of your space – do people trip over the same object constantly? If so, move it! Or do your friends avoid certain rooms, corners or chairs? Ask yourself why. Which is your most – or least – popular room, and why? Are there 'dead' zones in your home? Examine those rooms in terms of Five Element colours, shapes, temperatures and activities. Cats have a knack for finding the coolest spots in the summer and the warmest, cosiest spots in the winter, so watch where they curl up or stretch out.

Add space, dimension and an outlet to dead corners or dark passages, or walls at the end of passages, with sensitively placed lights, plants, mirrors and photographs or paintings of landscapes. Small fountains, fish tanks and potted plants all help to keep **Ki** humming. In traditional Japanese teahouse design, space is of paramount importance. Equally vital are translucent shoji screens or room dividers, so you are always aware of subtle shifts in light and season.

Space facilitates **Ki** movement. The exquisite *Book of Tea* gives some simple advice to help harmonise external and internal environments: a minimum of furniture; a carefully placed vase with seasonal flowers; a single branch of cherry blossoms in springtime, and please, don't rush over to sweep up those blossoms that drift gently to the floor. Leave them there. They reflect nature.

Let Your Garden Talk to You

Similarly, in your garden, create meandering, flowing and natural borders of wood or stone in your flower and vegetables beds. Avoid tight right angles, or straight paths. Remember **Ki** flows in wavy lines. Avoid cropping your lawns like a military-style haircut. Avoid dial-a-gardens where a team of gardeners arrive and plant beds in a twinkling of an eye according to some expert's advice. Let sections of the garden talk to you (like different rooms) and work on them in stages according to the slant of light, heat, shade and soil. Be conscious of the array of Five Element colours in your floral mix, to balance the predominantly green, desert, mountainous, or seaside landscape in which you live. Grow herbs in your flower bed and flowers in your herb bed. Leave some of the weeds there – they help to harness the soil and feed the bugs.

Arrange beds and seasonal plants and fragrances according to your windows, so you don't always have to go outside to enjoy a special rose bush or smell a bed of basil or mint, or enjoy the deepening reds of a tree in autumn. But don't have huge bushes blocking your views or trapping you in, or providing hiding places for burglars.

Choose perennials, plants and rock shapes that match your surroundings and water needs, so your personal environment flows into the natural environment. Gardens are very harmonising, as is gardening. I keep thinking of the healing effects of those magnificent gardens and soothing views surrounding many of the Swiss hospitals where I have taught or visited.

Inspire Your Kitchen and Workspace

Inside your home, apply the Five Elements to the function of each room. In your **Fire** room (your kitchen), your stove should not be side-by-side with your **Water** features like your sink and fridge, because this sets up contradictory forces. In the line-up of the Five Elements, **Wood** separates **Water** and **Fire**. Thus a wooden counter, cupboards or floor between stove and fridge, or stove and sink, enhance a creative **Ki** flow. **Fire** and **Earth** mix well in brick ovens, or in the traditionally grand old ceramic ovens built for baking bread and radiating luxurious warmth in a central area in many Swiss and German farmhouses. Food preparation is an **Earth** activity, with **Metal** providing chopping device and cooking pots, or **Water** providing the latter in glass pots.

Make sure you have a practical workspace, ideally with a view of a garden or something inspiring. In New York, I prepared my food on a wooden countertop facing window boxes filled to overflowing with colourful petunias and the butterflies and tiny birds they attracted during the hot summer months. Pots of cheerfully flowering red and pink begonia hung down from my tall ceilings in the winter. Similarly, I have always written my books facing a window with a view, from the noisy streets of London or New York, to the volatile streets of Jerusalem's Old City, to old wooden barns on a farm near Zurich, to ocean views off the rugged Cornish or Cape coast.

Views provide an acute sense of seasonal shifts, sights, smells and sounds, many of which have popped up in my texts throughout the years. Views also provide a link with the external world, vital for your Tao, vital for writers and others who spend long hours working in isolation. Have another look at my comments in Chapter 3 under the heading 'Ki *in Many Directions*' about Swiss architect Andre Studer and Florentine architect Renato Severino. In their different ways, each created wonderful

Architect Renato Severino's home in Greenwich, Connecticut, USA, maximises views and seasonal shifts via a creative use of windows and mirrors. He calls it an 'indoor/ outdoor house', where, he says, 'even a storm is beautiful!' (Photo © Renato Severino)

'indoor/outdoor' houses for themselves and their families. By maximising views of sky and natural scenery, the architects incorporate subtle shifts of light and season in their living and work spaces.

If your workspace has a lot of electronic equipment (computer, fax, printer, phones, etc.), balance this **Fire** activity with plants (**Wood**), ground it with some **Earth** textures and colours, maximise your windows (**Water**) and views, and keep your **Metal** filing trays or cabinets functional and free of clutter. **Fire** and **Wood** are good for inspiration and creativity; **Earth** for centring and focus; **Metal** for clarity and incisive thought; and **Water** for contemplation. Windlowless computer rooms lined with terminals are **Ki** cemeteries. They can be revitalised, however, by ensuring computer workers take regular breaks, especially outside or near a window, and by adding potted plants, mirrors and landscape scenes to the space.

Living Rooms and Dens

To plan a living area, also a **Fire** and **Earth** zone (the core of home and hearth), do a quick review of all your favourite living areas, and make a note of the recurring features. A living area is multifunctional, needing to provide a setting for good communication (**Fire** and **Metal**), comfort (**Fire** and **Earth**) and also solitude and contemplation (**Water**).

Avoid an excessive use of red or spiky shapes – people will find an overload of **Fire** too threatening. Add warmth to a cold room by (**Wood**) panelling the walls or by placing a dark, loamy brown (**Earth**) rug on the floor, or by scattering around handwoven ethnic rugs that invite you to curl up on them. Terracotta tiles (a mix of **Fire** and **Earth**) help to cool a warm room, with a richly inviting effect. If you work at home, avoid letting work papers spill over into your living or sleeping areas, or screen them off in some way if you're in cramped spaces in a big city. Whether large or small, your living area should have some central core (**Earth**), where people are drawn together, like a low table. 'Splashes of orange (**Earth**) also help to sustain conversation and connect the person to the place,' says Anne Gray.

Leather and all other animal skins represent **Fire**; a shiny satiny, or reflecting surface represents **Water**; handwoven textiles and rugs represent **Earth**; metal furniture or shelving or metallic objects represent **Metal**. Avoid an excess of one over the other.

Take another look at your living space. Does the TV dominate it? If TV numbs interaction and family conversation, move your set to a corner and place it in an 'entertainment centre' cabinet, so you can close the doors when it's not in use. Or drape a woven cloth over it. The TV is a constant **Fire** invasion. Avoid having a set in your bedroom, or wheel it out of sight before you fall asleep.

Make sure none of your chairs have their backs to a door, unless a mirror offers views of all who come and go. If one interior door faces another interior door, hang up a plant or place a plant on the floor between the doors.

Clear up clutter. Remember, it's stifling your **Metal** element, your flow of **Ki**. As I write these words I glance at the hopeless clutter on my desk and in my office. I'm surrounded by piles of 'undigested' papers and files and boxes. I feel an urgent need to listen to some of my own advice. I'll tackle the mess as soon as I finish this book . . .

World Kitchens

Meals inspired by the Five Elements are joyful, colourful affairs. They can also be very renewing for people who are cost conscious, but want to become more inventive and adventurous in their search for variety, eye appeal and better nutrition for their families.

Many different books have been written on cooking with the Five Elements, with assorted interpretations and variations according to their application to Chinese Medicine. But let's take a global overview and simplify everything to get to grips with some basics. To begin with, become more seasonally conscious. Relish the sight, taste and fragrance of each season, through seasonal foods and herbs. Spark your taste buds with seasonal textures and tastes to reduce a year-round reliance on fast, fatty, rich and deep fried foods.

Renew your awareness of local produce, especially through farmers' markets. Enjoy experimenting with the recipes and uses farmers often generously share with you. Even if you don't have a garden, grow your own herbs and sprout your own sprouts in a sunny window.

Prepare and cook your meals according to seasonal rhythms, advises Paul Pitchford in his book *Healing with Whole Foods*. Light, swiftly cooked young plants and greens, and fresh salads in **Spring**; lightly cooked meals with a dash of fiery, spicy flavours in **Summer**; sweeter, tan, yellow and golden squashes in **Late Summer**; root vegggies, baked or cooked slowly in the **Autumn**; and hearty casseroles and heavier grains cooked slowly in **Winter**.

Have some fun applying Five Element principles to the ethnic dishes in your family. Monique Jamet Hooker's *Cooking with the Seasons* is a celebration not only of her youth in Brittany but the seasonal variations in taste, source, texture and colour in her mother's kitchen. Recipes are spiked with wonderful family photos and anecdotes. My favourite from her collection is apricot tart – a great example of Late Summer in both colour and taste – and made out of a brisk seasonal fruit with a two-week peak. Apricots picked in the morning are made into jam that afternoon or dried for the winter months. The prettiest are saved for apricot tart. You can practically taste the sunshine and warmth in her recipe.

Monique Jamet Hooker's Apricot Tart

Take half a pound of fresh apricots. Halve them. Remove pits and save them. Crack pits, remove the nuts, break them into pieces and toast them in a pan over medium heat. Grind them in a food processor and keep them until later.

Cook the apricots with half a cup of sugar and three tablespoons of water for about five minutes, until they are slightly soft. Remove about half of the fruit. Keep this aside in a bowl. Continue cooking the rest for about another 10 minutes, until they are very soft. Purée these soft apricots, blend with ground nuts, vanilla, the grated peel of 1 lemon, the juice of 1 lemon and 3 eggs. Warm this mix for about five minutes – medium heat until thick – do not boil. Pour the purée into a pastry shell and decorate with the halves you kept aside. Place in fridge until ready to eat. You can also use the apricot filling (without pastry) over ice-cream.

As I mentioned in an earlier chapter, we've become so spoiled in our major cities with their array of international restaurants, and our year-round supply of Middle East or South African avocados, Hawaiian or Costa Rican pineapples, tropical mangoes, bananas and papaya, that we've become blasé. We've lost our seasonal edge. Which doesn't mean we must eliminate choice from our food and become boringly puritanical. Only that the Five Elements remind us of ways in which we can flow with the seasons, developing not only a new appreciation of local foods, but of ethnic dishes that match people, lifestyles and seasonal produce, and have evolved over generations.

Japan

Japanese cooking is intensely seasonal, not just in recipes, but in aesthetics, as a way of celebrating each season. My former teacher, and good friend, Pauline Sasaki remembers her Monday night family meal of *tempura* (veggies and shrimp lightly dipped in batter), and fresh *sashimi* if her father had time to go to the local fish market. Pauline was raised in Connecticut, USA by Japanese-born parents. To this day, she says the best *tempura* combo includes celery leaves, carrots, green peppers, onions, sweet potatoes (**bitter** and **sweet**), all dipped in a fish-based broth with freshly grated daikon (white radish – **pungent**). The drink of choice was good green tea, or *genmai* (rice tea). 'A very well-balanced meal,' says Sasaki, 'and it has influenced me to this day re ordering in a Japanese restaurant (who has time to cook?).'

Popular side dishes help balance the flavours of the main meal: **hot**, **spicy**, Japanese horseradish (*wasabi*) – but just a dab, as it explodes the mouth – a tiny bowl of soysauce (light and very **salty**, or thick, dark and less **salty**) and some sliced pickled ginger (**sour, pungent**). *Sashimi* (raw fish) must, for health reasons, be freshly caught and seasonal, as must the fish content of *sushi* (nori – seaweed wrapped rolls of rice, and a core of tiny chopped ingredients – very seasonal, with many vegetarian variations).

When I spent a couple of winters in the apple and cherry growing areas of the Okanagan Valley of British Columbia, Canada, I loved the idea of the root cellar lined with locally grown apples and vegetables harvested for the winter months. During the summer, boughs were heavy with a luscious array of pink, crimson and blood-red cherries, ranging in taste from tart, to slightly bitter, to intoxicatingly sweet. The warmth and taste of freshly picked cherries has ruined me for imported cherries ever since. My winters in Germany and Switzerland have made me love *feldsalat* (lamb's salad in Britain), (*nusslisalat* in Switzerland), a spinach-like vegetable abundantly available during the winter months, high in vitamins and capable of growing under the snow, but developing far too bitter a taste to be edible in the summer.

Cornwall

One of the special joys of growing up as the daughter of a Cornish mother, was our appreciation of Cornwall's national dish, the Cornish pasty, relished throughout the world wherever the Cornish settled, especially the hard rock mining areas of North and South America, South Africa and Australia. Originally a miner's food, a complete meal to nourish countless generations of tin miners through long shifts in deplorable conditions and 'built strong enough to survive a fall down a mine shaft' my mother used to say. The pasty evokes anecdotes throughout the Cornish diaspora. She used to tell me how families would smuggle freshly cooked pasties to their relatives in hospital to eat straight after surgery. My best memory is the sight of my mother chasing our family dog around the garden after he grabbed a slab of rumpsteak off the kitchen table when she was preparing pasties for a dinner party. She rescued the meat and duly completed her pasties.

My Mother's Cornish Pasty Recipe

Prepare your pastry in advance. Prepare your ingredients – all raw: a plate of sliced potatoes, a plate of chopped onions, and a plate of small chunks of rumpsteak. (As I am a vegetarian, my mother would use grated carrot, swede or parsnip instead of meat.)

Roll out the pastry and cut a shape about the size of a side plate for a modest pasty, or a large dinner plate for a really hefty appetite.

Place a good handful of potatoes in the centre of the pastry, a handful of onions on the potatoes and then a handful of rumpsteak chunks (or other

⟶

---

vegetables) on top. Shake plenty of pepper and salt over the ingredients and add a dab of butter. Then raise one edge of the pastry over the contents and 'crimp' it together with the opposite edge, to create a pasty shaped like a half moon. Make a small hole in the centre of the pasty to let out the steam. Whisk an egg in a side dish and brush this liberally over the pasty to give it a golden brown colour during cooking.

My mother always said cooking temperatures varied from country to country depending on climate, so use the same sort of temperature you would use for a meat pie. Or follow local guidelines from Cornwall – bake at 200°C (400°F, Gas Mark 6) for ten minutes, and then reduce heat to 190°C (375°F, Gas Mark 5) for about thirty-five minutes.

The density of veggies (with or without meat) gives a slightly sweetish flavour, spiked by salt and pepper. Though best suited to sustain you through a blustery winter day, the handy pasty is great to take on picnics in the summer time. I've also seen the Cornish-in-exile enjoying their pasty with gusto and a cold beer on a blisteringly hot tropical day. The *empanada* is believed to be a smaller, very local variation on pasties introduced originally to Bolivia's tin mining regions by Cornish miners.

A tossed salad provides a marvellous opportunity to experiment with Five Element colours and flavours. While grating fresh beetroot, onion and carrot, New Orleans artist Dennis Ruiz once told me he mixed all sorts of exciting colours together in his cooking just as he mixed colours on his canvasses. It's a great way to tackle a salad. Mix different dark and light greens together (**Wood**), add radishes, tomatoes and grated beetroot (**Fire**), yellow peppers and grated carrot (**Earth**), grated daikon (**Metal**), and some black beans (**Water**), and there's your Five Element palette.

You could achieve an equally colourful Five Element mix in a medley of vegetables, lightly sautéed or steamed to maintain their crispness and colours – courgette, broccoli, red peppers, carrots, yellow squash, potato, celery root and mushrooms.

If a flavour and a colour happen to match, you have an added bonus of course, as with millet. It's yellow, has a sweetish flavour and it is the grain associated with **Earth**. The coffee bean is actually red and bitter in flavour, a good **Fire** example.

Each element has an associated grain. Corn is **Fire**'s grain – and very popular in hot Mexican food. Traditionally, corn is a sacred crop for many Native Americans, especially the Hopi. Rice is **Metal**'s grain – a staple in the Orient, and a good balance for hot, spicy food; Beans, especially black beans, belong to **Water**, and provide an excellent substitute for meat in winter casseroles. Corn and beans (**Fire** and **Water**), provide a perfect balance and a popular combination in many Mexican dishes. Corn and beans also grow well together in the fields, as do a number of foods enjoyed together, like basil and tomatoes.

In terms of flavours, remember the line-up: **Wood** (sour); **Fire** (bitter); **Earth** (sweet); **Metal** (pungent): **Water** (salty). The art is to balance or combine flavours according to climate or individual need. Generally, **sweet** and **spicy** foods are warming, while **sour**, **bitter** and **salty** foods are cooling. There are other effects too. As herbal professor Dr Guoen Wang says, **sour** has an astringent effect, **bitter** eliminates, **spicy** decongests or disperses, **salty** can have a cathartic effect, and **sweet** expands, lubricates and warms.

Many foods or herbs combine different flavours, but may have an effect that doesn't match their flavour. A skilful practitioner of Chinese Medicine will help advise you as to the foods, herbs and flavours you require medicinally, according to whether your chronic or acute condition is dry, damp, hot or cold. Harriet Beinfield and Efrem Korngold's *Between Heaven and Earth – a Guide to Chinese Medicine*, has a great chapter on culinary alchemy.

Soybean products, like tofu and tempeh, are versatile and healthy products we vegetarians love. Bland, moistening, cooling foods, thus great for summer and dryness, they can be balanced according to season and need by hot or spicy seasoning and various imaginative flavours.

Mexico, New-Mex and Tex-Mex

In New Mexico, I was fascinated to see honey placed on the table during mealtimes. You are encouraged to dip a piece of soppapilla (puffy bread) in honey to cool the mouth, to balance the effect of a fiery, spicy chilli.

The varieties of regional Mexican dishes are endless, made vividly colourful with red, green and yellow peppers, tomatoes and cilantro, mouth-burning dark green jalapenos and a cooling guacamole. Although I left Mexico too young at four to have more than a memory of spicy frijoles constantly cooking on the stove, I have always appreciated the finest of Mexican foods, the more so since my recent return to Texas to live. The combined colours and tastes of many popular Mexican (and hotter Tex-Mex) dishes is pure Five Elements. This applies to the basics – beans and corn (**Water** and **Fire**), *guacamole*, (**Wood** and **Earth**), savoury rice (**Metal** and **Fire**), *tortillas* (flat bread, made from corn or wheat), and a fine *margarita* to cool you down (sour taste – **Wood**, and served in a glass rimmed with salt – **Water**.)

On a blisteringly hot day, there's nothing quite like blue corn chips dipped in a bowl of home-made salsa to quench the thirst (fresh tomatoes – (**sweet/sour/salty** – and very thirst quenching); cilantro (**bitter** and **cooling**), raw onion and black pepper (**pungent** and **heat dispersing**), a quick squeeze of lime (**bitter/sour** and **cooling**), fresh garlic (**pungent, de-toxing, heat dispersing**, thus **cooling**), and that special mix of herbs according to the restaurant or supplier.

India

Similarly, consider the range of Five Element flavours in the widely regional varieties of Indian cooking and spices. A classic, basic masala of mixed spices includes cardamom, cinnamon, cloves, black peppers and nutmeg, made extra spicy in some regions with the addition of coriander and cumin. Again, depending on the region, an Indian meal is spicy, but includes side dishes of **sweet**, **tangy** or **bitter** chutney, or all three, *raita* – yoghurt combined with **sweet** (banana), or **sour** (cucumber), or **bitter** (spinach) flavours. Yoghurt drinks can be plain, **sweet** (mango) or **salty**. So, an Indian meal is like a celebration of the Five Elements.

Pungent, spicy dishes are well suited to hot climates for a very simple reason. They warm you, so on a hot summer day you break out in a cooling sweat. **Spicy** foods also clear mucus and congestion from the system, great for constipation or nasal blocks and great for the **Metal** element's lung and large intestine connections.

South Africa

During my early years in polyethnic Cape Town, I was fascinated by the breadth and variety of Malaysian and Indian curries, some with side bowls of coconut and fresh banana (**sweet**), others with home-made chutneys of local fruits, and local curried fish dishes made from whatever was caught that day off the Cape's craggy coastline. My lingering memories of Cape Town are triggered by a fragrant mix of spices, salty air and hedges of flowering jasmine.

My friend Willy Naidoo, who grew up in Cape Town's beloved and densely polyethnic quarter of District Six (viciously levelled during the early 1960s by the apartheid government), used to tell me how her mother would buy spices from a local Indian spice dealer, and how curry could create a feast out of leftovers for a large, poor family. Willy showed me how to sauté the spices first, to entice their flavours, before adding onions and then other ingredients, lentils for daal (**sweet** and **pungent**) in one pot, and local vegetables in another pot. Willy serves her array of curries with a bowl of freshly chopped tomato and raw onion (very **cooling** and cleansing) and one of her home-made (**sweet**) mango chutneys. Note the differences in flavour between raw and cooked vegetables – the onion is considered pungent when raw, but sweetish when cooked.

Ukraine

Austin-based acupuncturist Alighta Averbukh, who was born in Odessa, Ukraine, and is also an accomplished chef, talks about her earliest memories of coming home from school and opening the door to the fragrance of borscht, and the sight of her grandmother stirring the pot over a gas stove. She emphasises the range of regional and seasonal variations of this all-time favourite. Alighta's winter variation of borscht is a nutritiously thick and complete meal – very different from the brilliant red soups I've sipped in restaurants in Berlin and London.

> ## Alighta's Borscht
> Sauté shredded beets, carrots and onions. Boil potatoes and cabbages in another pot. When the potatoes are ready, toss in the shredded beets, carrots and onions. Season with garlic, salt and pepper. Before serving add parsley and a dollop of sour cream. The cooked vegetables combine to give a **sweetish** flavour, very nourishing on a wintry day, balanced by **spicy**, **bitter** and **sour** tastes.

China

My colleagues and friends at the Academy of Oriental Medicine in Austin, Dr Jamie Wu and Dr He Yan Wu, invited a group of us for hotpot – a traditional favourite from their home province of Schezuan. This is like a Chinese fondue, except the pot is divided in the middle for yin broth and spices on one side, and Yang spices on the other side. The vegetables are all flavours according to season and availability.

Dairy products are taboo for most of my colleagues in Oriental Medicine, and I have certainly minimised my intake during the last couple of decades. But I have developed such a regional awareness from my global travels and a respect for national dishes, that I would never, for example, tell a Swiss patient to cut out cheese and chocolate – only to modify them, and realise their mucus-producing effect on the body. I advise my patients to choose rennetless cheese and organic milk products, free of artificial hormones.

Switzerland

However, there's nothing quite like a Swiss fondue to cheer the heart after hiking several hours through the snow in the mountains. Although it's a heavy meal, and no-one would want it every day, or during the summer, there are ways of making a fondue more digestible. Prepare it for lunch or early evening, and never for a late meal. You'll eat less if you balance it with a crisp green salad, which means you can also introduce some **bitter** and **sour** flavours and textures to balance the heavy **Metal** concentration of cheese. Choose a crusty bread – whole-wheat preferably, but not multigrain, that's too heavy. And serve hot tea (never cold drinks) to help you digest the cheese.

A popular cheese fondue mix in the Swiss German cantons, is grated Gruyère, Vacherin and Appenzeller – all strong, lusty cheeses. Emmantaler can be used instead of Appenzeller for a milder taste. But as Swiss German Bernadette Winiker tells me, each dairy has its secret mix and will prepare a bag of grated cheese for you.

Bernadette's Swiss Fondue

Plan on about 100–150 grams (about 3–5 oz) of grated cheese per person. Here's the recipe: rub your fondue bowl with garlic (pungent – and good for digestion). Heat the bowl on the stove and slowly add the cheese mix, then add a small bottle of dry white wine. When the mixture is nice and hot and starts binding, add a tablespoon of Cornstarch (**Fire**) and a shot of Kirsch (cherry liqueur, a delicate **bittersweet**). Keep stirring slowly and carefully, until the ingredients have bound to a smooth, creamy, thickish liquid. Take the pot to the table, where it's kept hot and bubbling on a burner. From now on, everybody helps you with the stirring by spearing a piece of bread on a fork and mixing the fondue with it. Don't rush it and, as the Swiss Germans say, '*E Guete!*'

Cooking with Herbs

Finally, one of my favourite dishes is pasta seasoned with fresh sage. We first tasted this exquisite dish in Cannero, Lago Maggiore, Northern Italy, near the Swiss Italian border. My friends Sonja and Klaus Jaussi picked a good handful of leafy twigs from a huge sage bush in a corner of their garden, sautéed it quickly, drained the pasta, and stirred in the sage. Delicious. Perfect for spring and summer, refreshingly pungent and bitter in taste, good for the liver, heart and digestion. In Chinese Medicine, the root is used for moving 'stagnant blood' in certain menstrual and heart disorders. In Germany and Switzerland, I got very used to drinking fresh sage tea for winter coughs and throat problems.

A Turkish pharmacist in Berlin's Kreuzberg quarter, told me that sage tea is served in many cafés in Turkey during winter time to help combat colds.

I try to grow sage wherever I live in the world. Plants from last year have spread into a beautiful bush in a sunny spot in my herb garden in Austin and we enjoy sage pasta at least once a week. A local, hardy, drought resistant variety of purple sage adorns the front of my house and rock garden. In the tradition of America's south west, I smoulder leaves of purple sage to cleanse the air of my home, especially my shiatsu room.

Learn something new about all the herbs you casually toss in your pot for flavouring. Instead of just using parsley as a garnish, try a salad combining different forms of parsley, and enjoy the slightly bitter, salty and cleansing flavours. Apart from tasting good, parsley is an excellent diuretic. You need very little space (window boxes or a tiny patch of garden) for parsley, sage, thyme, rosemary, oregano and basil, the basics. Acquire new seasonal uses for them, to appreciate the different Five Element tastes and benefits of each.

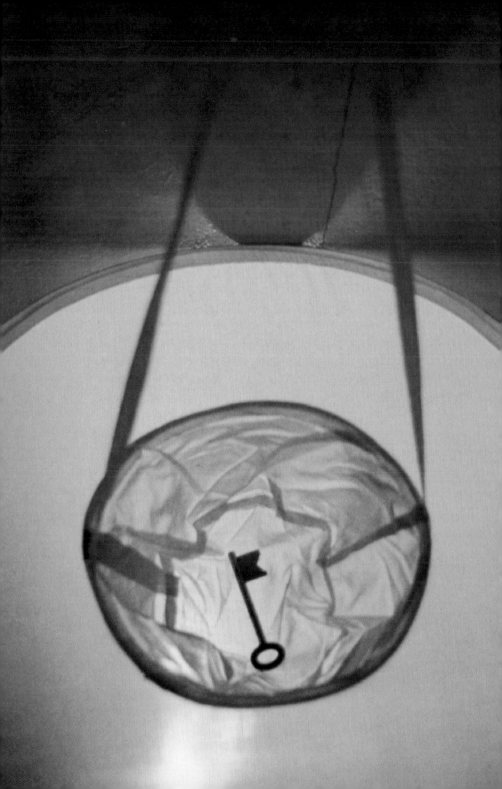

Chapter 6

Case Studies
and Cycles

◀ The Metal Element is symbolised by a
key in a white hat, one part of an
exhibition entitled 14 Hooks, 14 Hats,
5 Elements, by New York artist Jessica
Higgins. (Photo © Jessica Higgins)

Case Studies: The Six-Pack
Joe, Lisa, Angelika, Helene, Martin and David

Now I am going to take you through a number of case studies from around the globe, to see if you match any of their profiles, or if any of them sound like your loved ones, your boss, your ex-partner or current rival.

Wood: New York City

Joe was a top Wall Street executive in his mid-forties, and ex-military. I always knew when he was coming, because I could hear him barking on his portable phone as he jumped out of a cab and before he rang my door bell. He stepped into my therapy room with a military-type tendency to want to control and pace everything from the start. His first words to me were usually, 'I have to be out of here in exactly forty-five minutes.' Joe's muscles were snap tight. He brought so much static into my room that everything seemed to crackle when he changed into his sweatsuit.

Joe thought he was in great shape because he ran in the New York City marathon each year, and considered stretching 'for sissies', until he damaged a hamstring. Because of his business appointments, he usually ate very late at night, but came to me initially because of headaches, eyestrain and neck tension, caused, he said, by laptop overload while flying and at airports in between frequent business meetings. The headaches were beginning to interfere with his high octane performance.

Joe wanted a 'quick fix', which I told him wasn't possible. I suggested he join a gym to cross-train, to swim (he needed some **Water** sprinkled on his **Wood**) and to include some Tai Chi classes if they were offered, so he could learn about his breath and energy (a little **Metal** to thin out his **Wood**). I also advised him to arrange some early nights to balance his extremely driven, extremely Yang lifestyle. He rejected this as 'unworkable'. We talked about his late nights and he finally admitted something of an addiction to surfing the Internet as his only way of unwinding at night, following his divorce. As a compromise, I suggested switching his Zen Shiatsu sessions from the middle of the working day to the evening to help him sleep.

After a few weeks, he began to feel a change, and finally agreed to hire someone to teach Tai Chi and meditation classes in his offices. Within a month, Joe told me, he felt less headachy, and, 'Why the hell didn't you make those suggestions to me earlier?'

(Absolute) Fire: Boston

Lisa was a well-known artist in her mid-thirties who came to me initially because she was suffering from a creative block. She was normally a volatile, outspoken person, but had become withdrawn and isolated because of the block. This caused her a lot of anguish, as she feared she would never be able to paint again. I noticed she wore a lot of black and suggested she toss some red into her closet, and brighten up the room with some red flowers.

I worked on her **Heart** (one of the **Fire** meridians) and told her how the **Heart** meridian was also known as the ruler of the senses, and how it was the mechanism through which she absorbed and assimilated all the information she gathered through her senses. An artist's block, typically, is something of a shutdown in this area. The artist feels no impact, no resonance, no excitement, no interaction with the world. It's like a living death.

I also suggested she should coax her **Fire** with a little help from **Wood**, by walking through the park instead of taking the subway. And I suggested she should nourish them both with **Water** and her deep love of the ocean by taking long walks along the coast, regardless of the weather. After several weeks of sessions, she told me she had started to paint again. Her work was incredibly detailed, fine and time consuming. How honoured I felt when her return to her canvas included a work for me. It was large and dramatic. Bold splashes of red came bursting out of a solid black background. My work for her was done.

(Supplemental) Fire: Berlin

Angelika, an author, was going through a messy divorce. She asked if I would make a house call as she didn't feel like battling the streets of the city. Tall cranes spiked the sky outside her windows, as she lived on a corner close to one of Berlin's many reconstruction projects of the late 1990s. We closed all the windows to block out the noisy road drills and dust, and pulled down the blinds. But each time I tried to start the session, she complained of feeling cold, even though the place felt very warm and cosy. We moved the mat around from one room to the next, but she still complained of draughts. I ran around double-checking all the windows. I bunched towels and cushions under the doors. She still complained of draughts. Eventually, Angelika took her mat, crawled under a large antique desk and said, 'Ah, finally, a warm spot!'

I then realised it wasn't the temperature so much as her own feelings of vulnerability and insecurity that made her seek a dark 'nook'. So I crawled under the desk and improvised a few techniques so I could work comfortably on her there. It was a little like working in a dog kennel. She was expressing some typical **Heart Constrictor** meridian problems: divorce related vulnerabilities caused her to feel unprotected, cold, diminished. After the session, she told me all she wanted to do was to take a hot bath (**Fire** and **Water**) – a protective combination – and a way of nurturing or balancing the extremes in her life. She emerged from the bathroom looking invigorated. Later, she told me she used her renewed energy to tackle some problems she had been avoiding with her lawyer (**Wood**, between **Water** and **Fire**).

Earth: Montreal

Helene's father brought her to me originally when she was a teenager. She suffered from acute pain and migraines around the time of her menstruation. As it was only possible for me to work with Helene when I taught in the city, I offered to teach her father a few simple techniques to help ease her pain and discomfort. However, the moment he placed his hands on her shoulders, I could tell from her reaction that something was awry in their relationship.

During my next session alone with her, I shared my concerns with her. She told me her father had been sexually abusing her since the age of five. She felt she had no privacy at all in the family, except for those days when she was in such physical pain she could lock herself in her room.

Menstruation offered her a 'cave of privacy' as she put it. She also spent hours studying and reading and was determined to use education as a way out of the family.

Her mother had always been antagonistic toward her. Helene simply described this as a 'personality clash'. It was an appalling situation. Helene refused to take any sort of legal steps against her father, fearing the exposure, a shattered family and damage to her younger siblings.

Shortly after our conversation, she left home and backpacked around Europe (expressing her **Wood** and **Fire** elements) before starting university in Paris. She became a successful marathon runner, but admitted to me years later that she went through bouts of bulimia (also an **Earth** problem) to control her weight and maintain her running speed. Her love relationships have not been easy. She sees all the connections between her family experiences and her current problems. She shuns bodywork as 'too touchy-feely California', but found therapy a great help once she connected with a therapist who could match her sharp intellect. She has also worked hard and generously in recent years to repair the complex family situation (restoring **Earth**).

Metal: Zurich

Martin, a businessman, came to me originally because of severe breathing difficulties, caused, I could see, by excessive mucus. His nose was blocked, his complexion was doughy white and he always sounded as though he had a cold. He also suffered from frequent constipation.

'Martin,' I suggested, 'perhaps it would help if you cut down on milk and cheese?'

'But Pamela,' he wailed, 'I'm *Swiss!*'

We laughed about this, but he recognised the need for modifications in his diet. As we talked, he admitted he felt very depressed during autumn. He had a tendency to become inactive and withdrawn, which meant, in his words, a 'downward slide' into a long, gloomy winter (**Water**).

'Right,' I said, 'put your coat back on again. To hell with Zen Shiatsu today. Let's take a brisk walk along the Lake of Zurich and chat.'

It was one of those days when the silvery Lake had the timeless tranquillity of a Monet painting. The bathers of summer and late summer had gone. Yachts were anchored and covered, masts tilted gently against the white sky. Rowers in hooded sweatshirts moved rhythmically and effortlessly downlake, barely rippling the mirror-like surface.

But the beauty seemed to be lost on Martin. It was then he told me that the season had been a problem ever since he'd lost his 'centre', his **Earth** base, when he separated from his wife two autumns ago. 'It's as though I'm programmed to be depressed in autumn,' he said.

While walking, we discussed ways in which he could plan (**Wood**) well in advance, during the season he loved best, which happened to be summer (**Fire**), so he could look forward to a change of pace, like vacation time, or some new training courses he wanted to do, during the autumn. He could see the logic of this, and we discussed his options. He realised his physical problems worsened with inactivity. The day after we spoke, he told me he had decided to walk or cycle three miles to and from work each day instead of taking the tram, because, in his own words, he felt a need to 'experience my breath again.'

Water: London

David had just been discharged from hospital and asked if I could work on him at home. When he opened his front door, the first thing that hit me was the dark, inky atmosphere. His place had never felt like that before. He stood there wearing a navy blue sweatshirt and black sweatpants. This, too, was unusual. He normally wore bright, cheerful colours.

As we walked into his front room, I asked him two questions. 'David, has someone in your family died recently? And were you just hospitalised with a kidney problem?'

He looked at me, stunned. Yes, he'd recently lost his father. And yes, he had been hospitalised with pyelonephritis (infection of the kidneys and kidney girdle). How had I guessed? Had I suddenly turned into some sort of a clairvoyant?

I laughed, and explained a little of the Five Elements and the **Water** element, adding 'Your clothes and your inky flat told me everything.' David's profession? He was a veterinarian, but an offbeat character who often cycled around London doing house calls late at night, and worked until he dropped. I had warned him about 'healer's burn-out' in the past, but to little avail. His own body had found a way to slow him down.

During future visits, he admitted to me that work filled a gap following the death of his father, a gap he didn't know how to handle. I told him his flat always felt cold, and that means on-going misery in a city like London. We discussed ways in which his domestic situation could be more welcoming, without involving too much expense: some **Fire** solutions, more efficient heaters, warmer colours, red textiles and big cushions; some **Earth** solutions, warm soups sent up from the local deli when he didn't have time to cook for himself; long, hot showers and saunas at his neighbourhood YMCA so he didn't feel he was running up hot water bills at home. In short, his **Water**, and his **Metal** (grief) needed a spark of **Fire** and some nourishing **Earth**.

Do any of these case studies strike a chord in you? Do you recognise any loved ones? Are you beginning to see the interlocking patterns of balance and imbalance when one element shuts down, or dominates another, or is coaxed to support another?

The Four Cycles

Let's take a closer look at these patterns, and then see how our friends, Joe, Lisa, Angelika, Helene, Martin, and David, match the sequences of the Four Cycles. The easiest way to see how the Elements work within the grids of the **Four Cycles** is for us to take them on the road. The Four Cycles are:

- the Creative Cycle
- the Control Cycle
- the Over-Acting Cycle
- the Insulting Cycle

Let's Take the Elements on the Road

Imagine you're young and restless and your parents have given you a bright new sports car. You climb behind the wheel, switch on the ignition and zoom toward the motorway. That's your **Wood** phase.

Once on the motorway, you hit the top speed and roar past every other car in sight. That's your **Fire** phase. As you approach your exit, you begin to slow down, check your rear view mirror, the road, the conditions on the exit, and think about home and the meal you are about to cook. That's your **Earth** phase.

You slow down even more as you approach your home and drive slowly and carefully into your parking space. That's your **Metal** phase. You switch off the ignition and sit for a moment, sink into your seat and enjoy the silence of your new car. That's your **Water** phase.

Your adventure in your new car has taught you about (see page 134):

- *The First Cycle*, known as the **Creative** or **Generating Cycle** of the Five Elements, where one phase creates the next. We also call this the parent/child relationship. (Diagram A)

  But let's say your car breaks down as you approach home and you need a little help. You can't reach your parents, so you phone your grandparents.

  You now move into:

- *The Second Cycle*, known as the **Control** or **Restraint** (or **Back-Up**) **Cycle**.

  Your grandparents drive over with jumpleads. They are happy to help you, but in the friendliest of terms, they advise you to be a little less reckless. (Diagram B)

  You don't take any notice of them. 'Silly old people,' you tell your friends. What do they know about cars and young people today? Well, you underestimate your wily grandparents, and you are about to experience:

- *The Third Cycle*, known as the **Over-Acting Cycle**.

  Your grandparents watch you roar by. Later that day they come to your house and drive your car away and lock it in their garage. (Diagram C)

  You're enraged. To hell with them! Damn them! Now you move into:

- *The Fourth Cycle*, known as the **Insulting Cycle**.

    You phone your friends and go on the attack late at night. You smash the doors of your grandparents' garage and spraypaint 'Stupid Old Fools' on the walls. You and your friends climb into your car and roar off into the night. (Diagram D)

Cycles A and B are harmonious and creative.
Cycles C and D are discordant and injurious.

Let's take a more formal, and even closer, look at these cycles, their spin-offs and cross-checks, within the grand picture – the revolving circles of the Five Elements.

The Four Cycles In Depth

The Harmonious Sequences

1. Creative or Generating cycle (Diagram A)

This moves in a clockwise direction and in a perfectly logical sequence: **Spring** to **Summer** to **Indian Summer** to **Autumn** to **Winter** to **Spring**. One season creates the next, one season is the parent of the next season.

In terms of the Elements, **Wood** creates **Fire** when you light it, to produce heat; the end product is ash, one of the components of **Earth**, and **Earth** contains **Metal**, and **Metal** is one of the components of **Water**, and **Water** nourishes **Wood**, and so on. Ideally, this is a balanced arrangement. The compost heap in your garden offers a beautiful example. Rich earth results from the effects of moisture, heat, worms and bugs, on a decaying mix of leaves, clippings, table scraps, old vegetables, coffee grounds, tea leaves, etc.

The **Creative** (or **Generating**) cycle moves in a smooth, clockwise direction. However, the parent could dominate the child, or the child could sap too much energy from the parent, in an anti-clockwise sequence, causing a domino-effect of imbalances. This is why we need a **Back-up** or **Control cycle**.

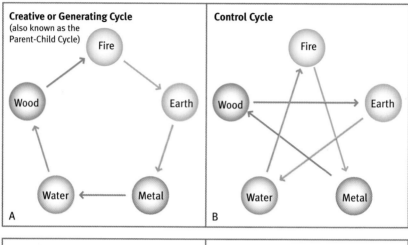

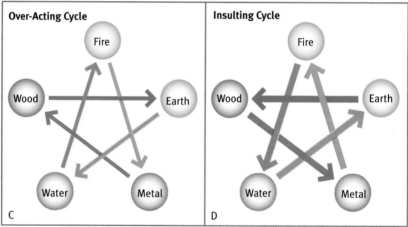

There are four major cycles in the five elements. 'A' is the creative, generating, or 'parent-child' cycle, the most harmonious. 'B' is the control (or 'back-up') cycle, also nicknamed the grandparent-grandchild cycle, a supportive cycle for 'A' whenever necessary, and equally harmonious. In 'C', the over-acting cycle, the grandparent becomes too dominating, too demanding resulting in 'D', the insulting (or rebellious) cycle, when grandchild rebels against grandparent and says 'Enough!'

2. The Control, or Back-up Cycle (Diagram B)

Should the creative or generating cycle run into snags or problems, there is a **Back-up**, also known as the grandparent/grandchild cycle. This is seen as a pentagram form within the grand circle.

- **Wood** controls **Earth** (example: forests prevent soil erosion)
- **Earth** controls **Water** (example: soil absorbs the monsoon floods)
- **Water** controls **Fire** (example: water controls a raging fire)
- **Fire** controls **Metal** (example: fire helps to soften and bend metal for tools and implements)
- **Metal** controls **Wood** (example: metal, in the form of an axe, helps to thin and prune an overgrown forest)

The Destructive Sequences

3. The Over-Acting cycle (Diagram C)

This occurs when the **Control Cycle** becomes excessive and over-powering, causing imbalances.

Wood over-acts on **Earth** (example: over-forestation robs the earth of nutrients)

- **Earth** over-acts on **Water** (example: excessive dam building can destroy a river's natural eco-system)
- **Water** over-acts on **Fire** (example: excessive flooding can destroy fires, heating systems, power lines)
- **Fire** over-acts on **Metal** (example: excessive heat will destroy metal along with everything else, as in the effect of a nuclear bomb)
- **Metal** over-acts on **Wood** (example: excessive axing of trees can damage the balance of the eco-system, as in the destructive clearance of the rain forest)

4. The Insulting Cycle (Diagram D)

In this sequence, the order of the previous (over-acting sequence) is reversed.

- **Earth** insults **Wood** (example: a devastating earthquake)
- **Water** insults **Earth** (example: over-flooding destroys the earth)
- **Wood** insults **Metal** (example: overforestation can rob the earth of minerals)
- **Metal** insults **Fire** (example: weapons of war can destroy production, power plants, power lines)
- **Fire** insults **Water** (example: excessive heat can dry up the river beds, or, as in the case of *El Nino*, can create warm currents in the ocean resulting in a cycle of global disasters.

Our Case Studies and their Sequences

Joe was such an excessive **Wood** and military type and so tight and controlling he left no room for love or warmth (**Fire**). He starved his **Earth** centre, (**Wood Over-acting** on **Earth**), which meant **Metal** and **Water** were left out in the cold, literally, causing great imbalances.

> **Solution:** Encourage **Water** in the **Creative Cycle** to modify **Wood**. Build up **Metal** in the **Control Cycle**, to thin out **Wood**. This means **Wood** will nourish instead of beating out **Fire** and **Fire** can nourish **Earth**.

Lisa's artistic **Fire** was out, literally. **Water** had come rushing in, **Over-reacting**. She wore black all the time and was scared she'd never paint again.

> **Solution:** **Wood** needed some action to coax **Fire** in the **Creative Cycle** and **Water** needed some **Control** from **Earth**.

Angelika's Fire was subdued by her pending divorce, and blocked all outer and inner change. **Water over-acted** leaving her cold and paranoiac and fearful of decisions and planning – **Wood**.

> **Solution:** Balance **Fire** in the **Creative Cycle** to centre her and motivate Earth to control and boost **Water**, resulting in a more productive relationship between **Water** and **Fire**, encouraging movement in **Wood**.

Helene's **Earth** centre was threatened and scorched by a destructive parent, throwing the whole creative cycle out of balance.

Solution: Helene left home, transforming **Wood** and **Fire** in the **Creative and Control** sequences to help her move away and re-establish her own centre (**Earth**), eventually enabling her to work on the **Earth** centre of her family.

Martin's **Metal** was cold and stuck in his sadness and loss, which meant **Metal** was having a negative effect on **Water**, and there was no impetus in the entire cycle.

Solution: Martin needed a roaring **Wood Fire** (**Creative** and **Control** **Cycles**) to move him, to motivate him to plan changes and to look ahead.

David's **Water** element was burnt-out which meant **Water** was unable to nurture **Wood** or **Control Fire**. The result was miserable.

Solution: David needed some help from **Earth** to boost (**Control**) **Water** to nourish **Wood** to create **Fire**.

What have you learnt about yourself? What have your learnt about yourself in the Five Element context of your family? Are you a **Water** person? Or a **Fire** person who needs a little more **Water**? Or are you overwhelmed by all your **Wood** associations, and need a little thinning out from the **Metal** element perhaps? Where are you in your **Earth** element? And what roles do your family members play? Do you all balance one another, or drain/or feed one another?

Contemplate this for a moment. If it helps, draw the Five Element circles and write the names of the members of your family in each relevant circle. Jot down anything else that comes to mind, like patterns of illness, addictions, professions, personality clashes, likes, dislikes, and so on.

This can help you study your family objectively, and even help you sort out some of those problems that crop up from time to time, especially at family gatherings. It can also help you trace cause-and-effect patterns in the family. And help you see the links in repeat patterns of behaviour, as in those of you who choose partners or spouses resembling one or other parent.

Chapter 7

The Five Elements
In Depth

◀ Although grief belongs to the **Metal**
Element, artist Karen Greathouse uses
all the Elements in her 'Homage to my
dead sister, Christiane'. (Christiane
died at twenty-five.) (Photo © Minh)

Wood

Spring/Green/Windy/Anger/Gall Bladder/Liver/Shouting/Eyes/Sight/ Tears/ Muscles and Tendons/Sour.

'She'd open her mouth and curse so powerfully I saw a green haze floating before my eyes.'

from 'Gimpel the Fool' by Isaac Bashevis Singer

I once met a man whose initials happened to be GB (our shorthand for gall bladder). When he came for a shiatsu session, he selected a green cover for the head pillow. I joked with him about being a textbook example of **Wood**. He looked astonished and said. 'You know, when I get really angry, my kids take me for a walk in the woods to calm me down!'

Let's see how the winds blow through this Element. Those of you who have read Michael Ondaatje's *The English Patient*, or those of you who saw the Oscar-winning film, were probably struck by the poetic way in which the author describes the mythic winds of North Africa and the Middle East in the first chapter. He talks about winds that are strong enough to bury armies in sand, or cause showers of red dust and blood coloured rain. That infamous spring wind, the *khamsin*, is very familiar to those of us who have spent time in the Middle East. Ondaatje writes, 'The *khamsin*, a dust in Egypt from March to May, named after the Arabic word for 'fifty', blooming for fifty days – the ninth plague of Egypt.'[1]

I can well remember suffering acutely from the effects of the *khamsin* after a press trip to the Sinai desert some years ago. I felt so headachy and weak my friends made me lie down in a room and drink masses of water. They soaked cheesecloth in water and hung it in the window to moisturise the impossibly dry, dusty air, a wonderful example of **Water** nourishing **Wood**.

As we noted in an earlier chapter, the world's assortment of different winds, mainly spring winds, and thus exquisite examples of **Wood**, can cause chronic headache patterns in local populations. There's the mythic

South-Easter wind in Cape Town. There's the *Föhn* in central Europe, and the Santa Ana of Los Angeles. Austrian author Robert Schneider writes about the ravages of the *Föhn* in his controversial novel and film, *Brother of Sleep*, published in some twenty-four different countries:

> The *Fohn* is roaring in the village, dancing like Satan, bending apple trees, breaking windows, plucking shingles from the roofs, burrowing in the haystacks and raising dust, furiously banging the shutters closed.

During the ravages of the dry *Föhn*, writes Schneider, no-one dares light a fire, not even a candle for prayer, for fear of engulfing the whole village in flames, a wonderfully graphic example of **Metal (dryness)**, over-acting on **Wood (wind)** producing a potentially threatening situation for **Fire**.

How well I remember the words of then British Prime Minister Harold Macmillan in 1960, when he spoke about the 'winds of change' blowing through Africa, referring to the steady dismantling of colonial rule. The **wind** aspect of **Wood** is one of its most dramatic features, and not only in terms of the chronic headaches (literal and metaphoric) it brings to towns and villages catching the brunt of its wrath. In Chinese Medicine, a 'windy condition' refers to a problem that jumps all over the body, like a wind 'striking shutters and bending apple trees', in Schneider's words.

Spring is a time of dramatic change, whirlwinds of change. An energising time for some, threatening to others, it's a powerful season, with plants bursting out of the soil and lambs out of ewes, a time when we throw open the windows and shutters, flex our muscles and move! The air is crisp, we feel a new vigour, we plan, we plant, we spring clean our homes and wash our windows.

Activist Green

Green is spring's colour, fresh, vital. Green is also a colour commonly found in the flags of various liberation movements. Think of the turn-of-the-century suffragette movement in Britain, with its distinctive purple green and white banners, posters, sashes, displayed at every march and meeting and protest. The colours were even used in curtains and tea sets.

Their explanation for the choice was very simple: green expressed change, white expressed purity, purple expressed nobility.

South Africa's ruling African National Congress used black, green and gold. In the years when the ANC was a banned liberation movement, and before democratic elections voted it in as the majority party, people found countless ways to express the banned colours in their clothing, art and even in their gardens.

The flag of Palestine is green, black, red and white. Green is also a sacred colour in Islam. Poetic references in the Koran promise the finest of green silks and brocades to believers who do good works. Years ago, a design company in London made a walloping mistake when it crafted a new logo and image for Pakistan Airlines and selected a green carpet for the aircraft. Devout Moslem passengers refused to walk on it!

In 'Paradise Lost: Tehran in the Springtime of Before' in the *International Herald Tribune* of 20 March 1996, Geneva-based journalist Nina Ingwersen writes about the Tehran of her youth, about the rituals of spring heralding the Persian New Year – *NoRouz*. 'Life was reborn once again,' she writes. She goes on to describe the elaborate process of spring cleaning and purchasing of new clothes and the growing of green shoots from wheat or lentils for the *Haft Seen*, a ceremonial table bearing a number of items symbolising abundance and renewal.

Think about Palm Sunday, such a symbol of the Holy Land in spring, with Easter just a week away. Biblical scholars now tell us that the graceful palms weren't merely a symbol of spring, but a symbol of Jewish resistance to Roman occupation. In fact, during the time of Jesus Christ, local coins bore a palm branch stamped over the image of the Roman Emperor[2] as a sign of protest. So Palm Sunday was something of a protest march.

Yet olive green is a colour we associate with the army, with symbols of power, and this is the danger when **Wood** becomes excessive. Power, anger, and control are all aspects of **Wood**, so watch out!

A policeman caught in a blustery south-easter wind in Cape Town is a perfect example of **wood**. Look how he displays his gall bladder meridian across his epaulets, down the side of his body and the stripe in his pants! (Photo © *Die Burger*, Cape Town)

During my early days of shiatsu training in New York, we were always told to beware of people with large, raised, big toes. This implies a tight **Liver** meridian, and someone who is full of anger, which reminds me of the day I noticed an interesting sculpture of a foot in the home of a psychiatrist friend in Zurich. The big toe was so huge, it stood almost perpendicular to the foot. I remarked 'If one of your patients created that, I am sure he or she is full of anger.' My psychiatrist friend nodded vigorously.

The **Gall Bladder** meridian runs down the sides of the body – where the stripes run down the sides of the trousers of many military, police and ceremonial uniforms. The **Gall Bladder** meridian also runs across the top of the shoulders like military epaulets. And just think of the number of countries choosing olive green for their military and/or police uniforms (the USA, Canada, Germany, to name a few). So we have some strong manifestations of the **Wood** elements in the power structures of several of our cultures. Olive green uniforms and vehicles of the German police give them a distinctly militaristic image.

Let's talk about the other manifestations of green and not leave a lasting impression of militaristic associations. Goethe chose green for the walls of his study, lovingly preserved in his former home, now the Goethe Museum in Frankfurt. A good choice for a creative mind always searching for new thoughts, fresh ideas. And all the more interesting considering his unique theories on colour, expressed in his *Farbenlehre*.

Eyes and Sight

As someone growing up short-sighted and astigmatic, I could never recognise people from afar. How often have I embarrassed myself by hanging out of taxi windows and frantically waving at bewildered strangers, thinking I knew them. Over the years I have learnt to recognise people by their gait and posture, which has sharpened my ability to diagnose patients from the way they walk, sit and move (all **Wood** characteristics) and generally express themselves through body language.

In 'The Case of the Colour-blind Painter' in his collection entitled *An Anthropologist on Mars*, Dr Oliver Sacks writes about one of his most fascinating cases, a famous artist who develops achromatopsia after a road accident (see Chapter 4, Experiencing the Five Elements). In Sack's story, the artist moves from agonising despair and a life-threatening inability to recognise traffic signals, to a creative exploration of his new black-grey-and-white world in his paintings and a heightened ability to experience the night. Oliver Sacks later expanded his fascination with the painter's experience, in *The Island of the Colourblind*, about (congenital) achromatopic islanders of the tiny Pacific atoll of Pingelap, who had extraordinary abilities to fish by night, because they could actually see the fish through the waves. *The Case of the Colourblind Painter* offers us another insight into the colour green. The painter was subjected to a Mondrian test, where light is filtered through narrow-band filters, to allow only long wave lengths (**red**), intermediate wavelengths (**green**) and short wavelengths (**blue**). The painter's contrast vision, and perception of form and boundaries, was so enhanced by the green filter, that he asked for a pair of glasses with green lenses!

Literature offers us another bizarre tale of green lenses, in *The Day He Himself Shall Wipe My Tears Away* by Nobel prizewinner Kenzaburo Oe of Japan. It is the surrealistic, disturbingly angry and painful ramblings of a man wearing green goggles while dying of liver cancer. The goggles distort everything, making even the leaves on the trees look as though 'they are always moving, even when the wind is still'.

I bought some Georgia O'Keeffe stamps while writing this chapter and was interested to read the quote the United States Postal Service selected for her red poppy stamps: 'Nobody sees a flower, really – it is so small – we haven't time, and to see takes time, like to have a friend takes time.'

To see, takes time. Our ability to *see*, on a profound level, implies depth, insight, perception, intuition, as does the expression 'to have a third eye'. But there is also an art, as my dear friend, New York chiropractor Dr Dick Kowal, once told me, in seeing in a detached sort of way, so as to protect the senses from becoming overloaded. In a healing context, this was especially important, he said, to enable the practitioner to see and hear the patients' problems, with compassion but detachment. In my own case, he felt my migraines would lessen if I consciously softened the overload I normally absorbed with my eyes. His advice (when I can remember it) really works.

Many of the older cultures have advised eating liver to enhance eyesight – both Hippocrates and Pliny advised this custom. Not much fun for a vegetarian, but a marvellous example of the **Wood** element. **Wood** is also logically associated with tears. Did you know that tears actually have different chemistries, depending on what prompts them – anger, sorrow, laughter or joy?

Gall and Gall Bladder

Monique Yantis, a French Canadian who lives in Austin where she is a laboratory technician (and an acupuncturist) told me that when she spins the serum of women who are on the pill, the colour turns green. She mentioned this in one of my classes after she heard me talk about the damaging effects of the birth pill on the gall bladder. It was only during the early 1980s that we began to hear about the high number of women who had their gall bladders removed after taking the Pill, especially if they took it during those early experimental 1960s and 1970s. Facts have long overtaken the old myth that gall bladders are only removed from women who are 'fair, fat and fifty'.

Finally, in an earlier chapter I mentioned how a range of languages share expressions associating liver or gall bladder with anger. Our strongest expression in English would probably be: 'Someone has the **gall** to do that'.

Here are the others:

German: *Seine Galle verspritzen* (literally, to spray gall); or to pour out venom; or the more expressive *Gift und Galle spucken* (to spit poison and gall). *Mir kommt die Galle hoch* (literally, 'I'm wretching on my gall', I'm very angry). *Mir läuft die Galle über* (literally, 'My gallbladder is overflowing', I'm livid). *gallig sein* – to be irritable. *Ist Dir eine Laüs über die Leber gelaufen?* (literally, 'Has a louse run over your liver?' Is something bugging you?).

French: *Décharger sa bile* (literally, 'to expel bile', to spew anger).

Dutch: *Zijn gal uitbraken* (literally, 'to vomit bile', to spew anger). *De gal loopt* (literally, 'his bile is running over', he's angry).

Italian: *Mangiarsi/rodersi il fegato* (literally, 'to eat/gnaw one's liver', to be consumed with anger). *Essere verde dalla bile* (literally, 'to be green from bile', to be very angry).

Spanish: *Querer uno comer a otro los hígados* (literally, 'to want to eat someone's liver', to be livid with rage). *Exaltarsele a uno la bilis* (literally 'one's bile runs over', one gets angry).

Fire

Summer/Red/Pink/Hot/Joy/Small Intestine/Heart/Triple Heater/Heart Constrictor/Laughter/Tongue/Speech/Sweat/Veins/Bitter

> Apparently in obedience to a local custom, the newly weds kissed every minute, kissed so vehemently that every time their lips made an explosive noise, I had a taste of oversweet raisins in my mouth, and got a spasm in my left calf. Their kisses did the varicose veins in my left leg no good. I can't tell you how much fresh caviar I ate and how much local red wine I drank. It's a wonder I didn't burst.
>
> *From Anton Chekov's letter to his sister Maria, 25 April 1887.*

The quote sums up Chekov as man and artist first, and medical doctor second, and provides a splendid array of **Fire** associations – love, the heart, joy, red wine, veins, and sensory overload. Treats and excesses. An Element that has so much positive imagery associated with it – a warm sensuous climate, the south, Flamenco dancers, passion, laughter and joy, also has its limits, its boundaries. If opera singers laugh too much, too loudly, they damage their singing voices, a fine example of an excessive **Fire** harming child **Earth** in the creative sequence. Similarly, if a person laughs hysterically and excessively, they can actually harm their heart organ. And anger can also damage the heart – a case of **Wood** overparenting **Fire**.

Art and Fire

But laughter is also a good boost to the immune system. Just the physical movement of the face and upturned mouth has a positive effect on the immune system. Laughter was used not only as an antidote, but as a skilful political tool by playwrights during South Africa's states of emergency. Censors actually believed the material wasn't a threat if people laughed at it. The irony of this helped create popular plays and shows that hit the world's top theatres with some of the most damning exposés of apartheid.

The performing arts offer us many marvellous examples of **Fire**. The Flamenco dance is such an expression of fire and passion in all its aspects, and of the **Fire** meridian (arm raised overhead, exposing the armpit). The French mime artist Marcel Marceau once performed a mime of death, where he raised his little finger (exposing the end of the heart meridian) and slowly bent over backwards in an arc, lowering his little finger to the floor.

In a very different context, Mikhail Baryshnikov celebrated his fiftieth birthday early in 1998 in a solo performance at New York's City Centre entitled 'Heartbeat: MB' in which he was wired up to an amplifier so the audience could actually hear the electrical impulses fired by his brain to his heart and muscles, and he could hear himself dance. He also wore red trousers. Many of his gestures exposed his Heart meridian, running through armpit to little finger. Commenting on a performance in Europe late in 1997, Baryshnikov said he wasn't nervous or puffing,

> . . . but my heart was beating probably 145 to 150 beats a minute. Your heart is very much connected to your mind. And that is what this piece is about, in general: the heart as a pumping instrument and the heart as all the old clichés about the heart, from ancient poetry to the modern medical tracts.[3]

Fire as Protector

In Chinese Medicine, this heart-mind connection is described as *Shen*. In shiatsu, we talk about the Heart meridian as the 'emperor of the senses'. **Fire** and its associated meridians play assorted roles, absorbing, processing and protecting, but there's always a threat lingering in having too much – or too little. **Fire** warms, protects and cheers us. As we have seen in an earlier chapter, the Heart Constrictor (or Pericardium) meridian protects the heart, amongst other functions. One of its major points is Heart Constrictor 8, in the palm of the hand where the second finger strikes when you clench your fist anxiously. The English translation of this point, appropriately, is Palace of Anxiety – reminding us of the Spanish expression *tener el corazón en un puño*, literally, 'to have one's heart in a fist', to be anxious.

When raging out of control, **Fire** can destroy. Volcanic eruptions can destroy entire communities, but because the lava is richly fertile, people keep returning to the areas, as around Agung in Indonesia, Mount Ruapehu in New Zealand, and, in time, is expected to happen on Montserrat, the emerald isle of the Caribbean recently devastated by eruptions. In Papua New Guinea, local legends explain the volcano and its eruptions to children, who grow up with no fear. Hollywood capitalised on our collective and insatiable need for the excitement and thrill of red hot lava bursting out of cone-shaped mountains in films like *Dante's Peak* and *Volcano*.

Passion and Excitement

Red excites, stimulates, tantalises. In English, we talk about 'seeing red' when our blood is up, when we are really angry, when there is a lot of **Wood** in our **Fire**. We also talk about 'spitting blood' when we are angry. We associate the expression blood, sweat and tears with Churchill's dramatic wartime speech in 1940, but the origin of the expression dates back to seventeenth century poet/priest John Donne.

Think of the difference between a warm, loving person in a bright red shirt (you love the red, want to cuddle that person), and an aggressively angry person in the identical bright red shirt (you hate that red, and want to back away from that person). No one can be neutral around red – it stirs the blood. Paint a room vivid red, and you won't be able to stay in it for a long time. I recall the story I saw on BBC TV some time ago about someone's tropical fish that became very excited and agitated each day between noon and 1.00pm except at weekends. The owner set up a monitoring system. After some days, she realised that the fish were reacting to the large bright red post office van that drove by the window each day at that time – except on the weekends.

In an earlier chapter, I mentioned the case of the achromatic woman who spoke about the unsettling effect red lenses have on her nervous system, which is interesting, as she has never actually seen the colour red. That red lenses can have an unsettling effect does not surprise me, it only emphasises the intensity of red's frequencies. It's the best colour choice for the AIDS ribbons – you spot it everywhere.

If you have cold hands and feet, wear red socks and gloves – never blue or black. If you get head colds, wear a red scarf or cap. Buy some soft red sheets and pyjamas if you want to be really cosy this winter. Countries associated with long snowy winters have red and white flags – Switzerland, Canada and Norway. One of advertising's most enduring success stories is the power of the red and white Coca-Cola logo. It is highly visible and recognisable all over the world and has been so for generations. During the 1998 Olympics, Coca Cola had an MTV-type commercial based on the theme of red. In German, *einen roten Faden haben* (literally, to keep a red thread running through something) means, to keep on track; the image of this reminds me of Boston's red line painted on paths and across streets to link major historic sites – especially those associated with the American Revolution.

The Dragon-Boat canoeing team of breast cancer survivors of Vancouver, BC Canada. Their pink T-shirts not only express the breast cancer movement, but 'Supplemental Fire' as a protector. Canoeing is a wonderful way of exercising meridians like Heart Constrictor, associated with breast health and post mastectomy work-outs. (Photo © Marina Dodis, Vancouver)

I associate pink more with Supplemental **Fire**, the protecting meridians of Heart Constrictor (protecting heart and circulation) and Triple Heater (controlling lymph and immune system, and body temperature). And pink is the colour associated with the breast cancer movement – pink ribbons and T-shirts, especially the logo and T-shirts associated with the *Dragon Boat* canoeing team of breast cancer survivors in British Columbia, Canada. Appropriately, dragon boat racing is rooted in an ancient Chinese legend where teams must row from the north (death) to the south (life) in search of the sprit of poet Qu Yuan (*Chatelaine*, October 1997). Earlier, I mentioned the role of both Stomach and Spleen meridians in breast health; the Heart Constrictor meridian also runs through the upper outer quadrant of the breasts (where most tumours occur), and of course good upper body circulation and good lymph circulation is of paramount importance to breast health and following a mastectomy.

Fire Foods and Drinks

Hot countries invariably have assorted spicy (**Metal**) foods but with balancing flavours and tastes to cool the mouth. Such countries enjoy a range of bitter red or pink drinks, like pink gin (gin and angostora), a great favourite of the British in the tropics, and other Mediterranean favourites like red vermouth and bitter san pellegrino. Coffee (originally from Ethiopia) is a classically bitter drink – and coffee beans are actually red. Caffeine is, of course, a stimulant found in assorted strengths in tea, cocoa and coffee, and consumed in varying ways according to different cultures. The tradition of strong tea in Britain follows the British worldwide at all times of day and night and in all seasons. It warms in the winter and cools in the summer and the ritual is a national characteristic. I was brought up on the cult of whistling kettles and scaldingly hot, strong tea, from the rugged misty cliffs of a Cornish winter to the heat of an African or Texan midsummer. I was raised believing most problems could be solved after a brisk walk and a strong cup of tea (a nice blend of **Wood** and **Fire**).

Head further east to Russia and many of the former Soviet states for the samovar tradition and even stronger tea, where the bitter taste is often balanced with intensely sweet candies, sugar lumps or biscuits, a reminder of our English expression bittersweet, and a balancing relationship between **Fire** and **Earth**.

Tea has also been applied as a salve for burns, and is currently being researched as a form of prevention against skin cancer.[4]

Fire Idioms

Interestingly, considering the relatively modern association of red with the Communist party (and expressions about liberalism), the Russians have many expressions associating red with bitterness and deception. 'A redheaded person is not to be trusted' is one example (*riizhii da krasnii chelovek opasnii*). Also, 'beware of someone who looks OK, but they're liars' (literally, 'a red field of rye, but the speech is all lies', *krasnoe pole rozhiu, a rech lozhin*). Similarly, appearances are deceptive (literally, 'a beautiful red berry has a bitter taste', *Krasivaya krasnaya yagodka, da na vkoos gorka*.

The ancient Hindu myth of **Fire** requires a wife to pass through fire to prove her fidelity to her husband. If she burns, she's guilty. Traditional and modern versions of the ritual were entwined in a highly controversial film produced in India in the late 1990s entitled *Fire*. In the film two brothers neglect their wives (one for a guru, the other for a mistress), and it is the wives who survive fire (literal and metaphoric) to run off together.

Your **Fire** element controls your speech, your tongue, the way you use language, those moments when you are tongue-tied, stutter, or cannot stop talking or giggling. I remember how my friends and I used to make church pews shudder with our hysterical giggling during our schooldays. Today, I'd examine one of your **Fire** meridians if you laughed for no reason, or if you suddenly started to laugh during a shiatsu session. Or if you couldn't laugh at all, like one of those stone-faced people who sit unmoved at a talk or play when the entire audience is screaming with laughter.

In diagnosis, the tip of the tongue reflects heart imbalances. Think of our expression 'something is on the tip of my tongue' when you want to express something but it just won't come out. The Italians have a good expression linking several **Fire** characteristics: *parole di sapore amaro*, 'words with a bitter taste'. So do the French, in *langue de feu*, 'a tongue of fire', as do the German expressions Zungenfertig (literally, 'tongue-skilled', eloquent), and *ein falscher Zungenschlag* (literally, '*a wrong tongue beat*', a slip of the tongue).

The French language also gives us some fine examples of the supportive relationship between parent **Fire** and offspring **Earth** in the creative cycle: *donner du cœur au ventre à quelqu'un* (literally, '*to give heart to someone's belly*', to cheer someone up) and *avoir du cœur au ventre* (literally, '*to have heart in the belly*', to have guts/courage).

Earth

Late Summer/Yellow, Orange, Brown, Khaki, Gold/Damp/Compassion/ Worry/Stomach/Spleen/Singing/Mouth/Taste/Saliva/Flesh/Sweet

> At the end of the season, soybeans seem to lose all sense of individuality. Turning from deep green to brilliant yellow to an indescribable shade of red-brown, they all blur into each other and sink back toward the earth, forming an upholstered surface that invites one to walk in and lie down.

> *From Chapter 'EARTH' in Living Downstream – An Ecologist Looks at Cancer and the Environment by Sandra Steingraber*

Soybeans and soya products such as tofu, generally high in a traditional Japanese diet, are considered to be one of the reasons why Japanese women suffer far less breast cancer, and far fewer of the symptoms associated with menopause (like hot flushes), suffered by Western women. However, as Sandra Steingraber reminds us in her book, corn and soybeans jointly account for the majority of all pesticides used in the USA. Make sure your soy products are organic.

Golden Octobers

Oh what a gift! As I write these words, my mind lingers on the Indian Summer of 1997 I experienced during my teaching trips in western

Europe, and a breathtaking train journey up the Rhine from Basel to Dusseldorf. Such beauty. Such clarity of light. Such an abundance of flowers everywhere, cascading out of windowboxes and tumbling over garden fences, and grape arbours weighed down by bunches of succulent grapes. A brief intake of breath before an abundant harvest. And yes, the outdoor cafes buzzed until late into the balmy nights, as people enjoyed the deliciously sweet, dark red sauser (when the grape juice has just started to ferment) typical of this season, and very popular in Switzerland, southern Germany and Austria.

I recall New York in a similar October, of 1987. It was the week after my surgery for breast cancer, when the city experienced a glorious Indian Summer, just for me, I thought. The air was vibrantly golden and I had never seen such an array of yellow and golden leaves fluttering above my head. I used to walk through the park each afternoon to listen to the violinist play near the bronze sculptures of characters out of Hans Christian Anderson. There was something about the quality of sound in those weeks that hit me with the same lingering intensity as the Indian Summer light. Yes, losing a breast was very much a part of an expression of Earth. Earth meridians run through the breast, are directly involved with breast function, and mythic symbolism of nurturing, sexuality and reproduction.

Earth has played a variety of roles in my own life. During my early childhood years in Cornwall, how well I remember those difficult months when my mother went through a nervous breakdown. Our family physician suggested she walk barefoot across newly ploughed fields. This wasn't difficult to do, as we lived in the midst of a farming community.

I have heard it said that many people yearn to return to the land of their birth when they are close to death. My mother was no exception. Even though she lived in Africa most of her life, she yearned to return to Cornwall to die. As this wasn't possible, I arranged to have her name placed on her beloved grandmother's grave in St Euny's parish churchyard of her home town of Redruth, Cornwall. She loved yellow roses. As a tribute to her I gave her old school friends yellow rosebushes to plant in their Cornish gardens in her memory. Yellow is a strong colour

Mother and Child in earth colours of gold and orange. Copper Canyon, Mexico. (Photo © Nancy Scanlan)

in Cornwall, from the abundance of yellow furze, a tough, sweet, coconut-scented briar-like bush dominating the hedges each spring, to the mustard-yellow moss growing on thousands of gray slate roofs.

Earth is also a balancing factor between each season, or an expression of that pause, that plateau hovering between the peak of one season and the slow descent into the next, a time when everything seems to stand still. **Earth** is also a balancing factor in your health and your life.

Earth and Rain Forests

When we think about **Earth** and its associations with centre, and dampness, our minds focus on the rain forests and the delicate, ecological balance we are destroying as we burn our rain forests at a rate of a football field a minute. During my time in the cloud forests of Monteverde, Costa Rica, during 1994, I was struck by the complexity of interdependent ecosystems that flourish there in the intensely damp air. And I experienced the special magic of double rainbows. Costa Rica practises more rain forest conservation than any other nation, and it is easy to see why. I was appalled by the devastating consequences of random clearances to make way for cattle grazing in the past. In the mountains, you can see deeply rutted scars left by successive cattle drives, and pitiful fields struggling to regain grasses after harsh clearances. In the valleys, the sheer volume of rain and moisture is so huge, that without the various ecosystems intricately designed to absorb this, the bare ground turns swiftly into a stinking, mosquito-infested swamp.

Aware of all this, a group of ecology-minded teachers and parents created a unique and totally bilingual (Spanish/English) Cloud Forest school in Monteverde, where all subjects are taught around cloud forest themes (a spider web as a theme for a geometry lesson, for example). The purpose is to inspire the kids to become the rain forest conservationists and environmentalists of the twenty-first century.

Earth Yourselves

We talk about someone being 'earthed' or 'grounded'. In our treatment procedures, we may work on one or other of the **Earth** meridians for precisely this purpose, to ground the patient, stabilise them, especially if they have just been through some emotional upheaval. If patients avoid **Earth** colours, I advise them to select fresh flowers in such colours, or to consider earth tones when they choose new furnishings or textiles for their homes. Again, furniture designer and antique restorer, Sophie Keir, co-founder of the Creative Edge, New York, whose work has been featured in *Architectural Digest*, says she has no problems selling little breakfast tables in yellow. However, she would find it impossible to move the same tables painted pink. As yellow is associated with nourishment, reproduction and happy families in the Five Elements, is this surprising?

Remember OJ Simpson's lengthy, Hollywood-style court case played to the world's TV in the mid-1990s? Remember the first day his flamboyant defence team presented its case? Members of OJ Simpson's family, his wheelchair-bound mother, his sister, his children from a previous marriage and other family members, all trooped into court wearing different shades of yellow. Perhaps the defence lawyers just wanted to ensure high and constant visibility for OJ's supportive family members for the court, the media and millions of TV viewers. We don't know what experts the defence team consulted. But in Five Element terms, it chose the colour most associated with family and nourishment. The ironic message was not lost on those of us in Oriental Medicine.

Vincent Van Gogh used a lot of yellow in his painting. Was this his subconscious way of trying to earth himself in the increasingly chaotic and disordered world of his alcoholism and madness? Think of his magnificent study of sunflowers. Not a surprising choice to anyone familiar with the acre upon acre of glorious sunflower fields that dazzle the eye and mind on a journey through the countryside in the south of France. But I often think about the predominance of yellow and other earthtones in his 'Artist's Bedroom' – bed, floor, sheets, chairs, pictures on the wall, washstand and parallel stripes in the view from the window. Vassily Kandinsky was once supposed to have said 'Yellow is the typically earthy colour. An intermixture of blue makes it a sickly colour. It may be paralleled in human nature with madness, not with melancholy.'[5]

Two paradoxical uses of the colour yellow, one sinister, one benign, came from South Africa during the late 1980s state-of-emergency, the finale of the draconian apartheid system. Police often drove around in a huge yellow armoured vehicle nicknamed 'yellow mellow' by the people. The particular shade of yellow was designed to blend with the sort of vibrant Cape light that has endeared the city to generations of artists. So the vehicle could creep up on you in a less threatening, less obvious form than if it had been painted olive green. Or, as someone said, 'It looked like a big version of a kid's toy.' When African National Congress activist Jenny Schreiner was in solitary confinement and subjected to daily interrogation, she grounded herself by decorating her prison cell with yellow scarves. She chose yellow to create order in a chaotic world. Schreiner is now on the personal staff of Nelson Mandela.

Earth meridians of Stomach and Spleen reflect the way we deal with cycles in our lives, and the lives of our loved ones. Nourishment and Reproduction are the key words. In short, **Earth** determines how we perpetuate ourselves, how we survive and reproduce ourselves, how we nurture ourselves and others in our families and extended families. We talk about Mother Earth types among our friends and colleagues. (What happened to Father Earth? Why do we only associate the Earth with women? Only traditional cultures talk about Father Sky and Mother Earth.) When the nurturing is excessive, we talk about 'smothering'.

When teaching the **Earth** element I don't just dwell on the female cycle, but hit the male cycle, too. What a taboo subject, rarely addressed in either Western or Eastern medicine. And I am not talking about the male menopause!

If women's bodies are subjected to cycles and rhythms, why not men's bodies? Whenever I throw this topic into my classes, my students react with amazement, surprise, and then nod in agreement, as though we have touched on something that is all too logical, but rarely discussed. The response from many of my male students has been one of wonder and relief that finally, someone has acknowledged something they have felt but been too shy to express. One of my students in Texas said he used to keep a journal to chronicle the cyclical changes in his body. Then he became so embarrassed about someone reading the material and thinking he might be crazy, he destroyed the journal. When he told us this in class, we all regretted that taboos had prompted him to destroy some invaluable insights. We encouraged him to start afresh.

I first became aware of the male cycle at the age of eleven when my fourteen-year-old middle brother Neil suddenly announced to me one day that his nipples got hard and painful at a certain time each month. 'Girls are told what to expect when they first menstruate,' he argued. 'But nobody talks to us about the monthly changes in our bodies.'

Male students, patients and friends have talked to me freely about the cyclical changes they experience. Here are some of them:

- changes in the toughness of their beards when they shave
- changes in their bodily smells
- changes in their emissions, whether ejaculations, or sweat

- mood changes
- moments when they feel so sensitive and aware, or, as one student told me, he could cry 'just watching a leaf twirling in the breeze'
- moments when they want to be close to someone
- moments when they want absolute solitude.

Some men tell me they are often most aware of their cycles when they are deeply connected to a lover (male or female). Another student told me he was so connected to his girlfriend, and so in touch with his own body, he could actually feel the exact time when she had a miscarriage, even though they were in different cities. Alas, only really enlightened parents raise their children – boys as well as girls – with this kind of awareness and consciousness.

Mouthing Off

Earth is also connected to your mouth, sense of taste and saliva. 'Mouthing off' or 'a big mouth' are popular expressions in a number of languages, implying someone who talks too much. Ever see someone with an over-active mouth who seems to chew their words in front of you? Or someone who spits all over you and makes you want to back away? Pimples at the corners of the mouth also reflect **Earth** imbalances, as does a tendency to have too much or too little saliva in the mouth. (However, the saliva problems can be caused by medications prescribed for psychiatric disorders.)

Taste and smell often go together (**Earth** produces **Metal** in the creative cycle). Which is why food seems so tasteless when you have a cold and lose your sense of smell. Or, why people who give up smoking often re-discover their sense of taste! Taste can often be used as a diagnostic tool – be conscious of the taste in your mouth as you read these words – is it sour, bitter, sweet, spicy, or salty?

Metal

Autumn/White/Grey/Dry/Melancholy/Large Intestine/Lung/Nose/Weeping
/Smell Skin/Mucus/Pungent

The sweet smell of plums, boiling in a huge copper vat, mingled
with the dry scent of Autumn to mark the start of another yearly ritual
in the life of a small Serbian farming village. They drink Slivovitz in
shot glasses and sing sad folk songs of past defeats and lost lives.

'To Wash down the Serbian Autumn, Plum Brandy'
in the New York Times, 31 October 1997

I first became aware of the appalling health consequences of the mining
industry at the tender age of nine as my grandfather lay wasting away
from silicosis. A former champion Cornish wrestler, he became so
disgusted with his diminishing body, he sat in the bathtub around 5.00am
one cold rainy winter morning and slashed his wrists with a razor. Like
thousands of Cornishmen, he went underground in the tin mines as a
teenage boy, and then had to travel to the mines of Africa and the Far East
early in the twentieth century, when the Cornish tin mining industry was
closing down.

Thinking back, I realise we were among countless families who grew up
before class action suits and industrial liabilities surrounded diseases like
asbestosis, for example; we accepted the devastating consequences of
mining as part of a miner's life (or death). Not just silicosis, and an array
of other toxic air related diseases, but the deaths, disabilities and
dismemberings that followed shaft collapses, blasting accidents and rock
falls. There is even a long narrow stone built at St Euny's churchgate, in
the heart of the former mining hub of Redruth, Cornwall, my mother's
hometown, to hold the multiple coffins following frequent local mining
accidents.

The mining industry is like a microcosm of the **Metal** element. The
meridians and organs associated with **Metal**, the Lung and the Large
Intestine, are especially vulnerable to environmental toxicants. Interestingly,

according to acupuncture professor Dr Jamie Wu, the Lung and Large Intestine are also the major source of health problems in Chinese Medicine. According to Needleman and Landrigan's *Raising Children Toxic Free*, children's lungs and large intestines are a lot more vulnerable than adults. Children absorb almost half the lead they swallow, while adults absorb about a tenth.

Not only did my maternal grandfather waste away from silicosis, but my uncle (his son) died of lung cancer; he was a heavy smoker, who went down the mines as a young teenager. My geologist father experienced colon cancer and my mother experienced cancer of the nose – all **Metal** cancers. The **Metal** element is also associated with a sense of separation, another sad fact of life in mining, where, traditionally, families have experienced long months of separation as the men travelled vast distances away from home, often to Godforsaken places, in order to work.

Metal and Nostalgia

Mining songs are invariably about sadness, loneliness and separation, another common theme in my own family. My maternal grandfather and great-grandfather spent years separated from their families. My geologist father spent years in the bush. Even before my parents divorced, I saw little of him. How well I can relate to patients who suffer from separation anxieties, especially those that seem to have no logical explanation or base, but to me suggest a **Metal** imbalance.

Seasonally, **Metal** is associated with Autumn, specifically late Autumn. **Metal** days are those days when you look out of your window and everything is overcast, grey, bleak. The air is becoming dry and sharp. Branches are bare against the stark white sky. Leaves crackle and scatter underfoot. It's a melancholy time. Summer is long over, Indian Summer has retreated, and many people dread the approach of a long, isolating winter – more so in the north than in the south, of course. Autumn can also bring a flurry of new allergies.

When I first taught in Switzerland in the early 1980s, my students told me that tuberculosis was once known as the 'disease of melancholy', possibly echoing a somewhat romantic view from the past often reflected in operas like Puccini's *La Bohème*. Melancholy, sadness, or grief also happen to be the emotions associated with the **Metal** element.

All the seasons, but especially **Earth** and **Metal,** are also exquisitely entwined in the opening page of Truman Capote's *The Grass Harp*:

> Below the field grows a field of high Indian grass that changes colour with the seasons: go see it in the fall, late September, when it has gone red as sunset, when scarlet shadows like firelight breeze over it and the autumn winds strum on its dry leaves sighing human music, a harp of voices.

Pungent Metal

Foods associated with **Metal** are spicy and pungent, like curries and hot Mexican food, both appropriate for hot climates. Both certainly have a cleansing effect on the intestines, as well as on nasal and sinus congestion! But a meal of curry includes a number of balancing tastes, based on local spices, vegetables and fruit, according to regional differences, as I mentioned in Chapter 5. Curries are hymns to the Five Elements, with tamarind (sour – **Wood**), yoghurt-based drinks (either sweet – **Earth**, or salty – **Water**), sweet mango chutney (**Earth**), or a bitter ginger chutney (**Fire**) to balance a hot curry that makes you cry, and with plenty of rice (**Metal**) to balance the feast in taste and texture. There's also a very practical side to rice (**Metal**). Rice water replenishes vital electrolytes depleted by dysentery.

Life and Death

The **Metal** colours of white and grey mean different things in different cultures. White is a symbol of life – and of death. In classical Rome and Greece, white symbolised life-beyond-death. It is the colour of mourning in the Orient. My Palestinian friend Karimah Tarazi, who lives in New York, told me about an embarrassing moment when she wrapped a wedding present in white for a Chinese friend. 'No, no,' said the bride's mother, hastily snatching the gift away before her daughter could see it. 'White is for *funerals*, Karimah. Go buy some red paper and wrap it up again!' This makes a lot of sense in the Five Elements. **Metal** (white) is fall, the dying off of Late Summer, and preparation for the hibernation of winter (**Water**). Red (**Fire**) symbolises passion!

In the West, we associate white with purity, the traditional colour of weddings, baptismal robes, confirmation, ascension, all familiar Christian rituals. For the Hindus, it means pure consciousness. For the Egyptians, the combination of white and green means joy.

I once bought a multicoloured spinning top from Berlin's Bauhaus Museum. When you spin it across the bare floor, all the colours merge into white. Similarly, Sir Isaac Newton's experimental way of passing sunlight through a prism resulted in a splash of seven colours, violet, indigo, blue, green, yellow, orange and red, all of which produced white when passed through a second prism. As the **Metal** element is associated with the intake of fresh **Ki** and expulsion of stagnant **Ki**, the energy of all living systems, the colour white as a collective of all the other colours, gives you a more comprehensive idea of the multilayered functions of **Ki**.

The Nose

We absorb **Ki** – and a lot more from the universe – through our nose and skin. Animals use their noses (just watch their nostrils twitching) to assess a room, another animal, you, danger, or safety. Where in English we would say 'we cannot stand someone' if we don't like that person, in German you say you can't 'smell' them, *jemanden nicht riechen können*, (literally, *you cannot stand their smell*). Hamburg-born Ute Schwarzer said if someone made her father really angry he would say, 'Do you want to smell my fist (bud)?' Both German and English share similar expressions, such as 'nosy' (*naseweis*), and, 'not to be able to see beyond the end of one's nose' (*nicht weiter als seine Nase sehen können*) and to be haughty ('nose stuck in the air', *die Nase hoch tragen*). In journalism, our highest praise for colleagues was 'they have a good nose for news' or 'they can certainly sniff out a good story'. The German word for rumour, *Gerücht*, is from the same root as *Geruch* – smell, hence the term *Gerüchteküche*, 'gossip kitchen', referring to a place or group of people stirring up gossip.

The nose is central to us – to our appearance, and to our instincts. Read Nikolai Gogol's *The Nose* for an absurdly comical piece of satire about a pompous bureaucrat whose nose is cut off by mistake by his drunken barber. When man and nose meet in the street, the nose denies he even belongs to the bureaucrat: 'My dear fellow, you are mistaken. I am a person in my own right.'

In English, if we dislike someone we sometimes say 'they make our skin crawl'. In Danish *hun er hudløs over for kritik* (literally, *'she is skinless when criticised'*) means, she is sensitive to criticism. In English, we talk about someone being thick or thin-skinned (insensitive/or sensitive). Our expression 'to save your skin' translates as *seine Haut retten* in German. To risk your life (skin) for someone or something translates as *seine Haut zu Markte tragen*. All of the above express the skin as our outer protective covering, another strong feature of **Metal**. Indeed, one of the most dramatic exhibits in the controversial exhibition on anatomy held in Mannheim, Germany, early in 1998, was the man holding his entire skin aloft like a diver's body suit. It has inspired me to hold up a long winter coat in my classes whenever I talk about the skin and the **Metal** element.

Water

Winter/Black/Blue/Cold/Fear/Trauma/Bladder/Kidney/Ears/Weeping/Hearing/ Bones Urine/Salty

> On the contrary, the water, which is the noblest of elements, does, of course, go all through the earth, so that our planet really floats in the ether, like a soapbubble, and there, on the other hemisphere, a ship sails, with which I have got to keep pace.
>
> *From* The Blue Jar *by Isak Dinesen*

Isak Dinesen was the pseudonym of Danish writer Karen von Blixen, best known for *Out of Africa*. The quote comes from a wry short story, something of a little parable, not only of the **Water** element, but of

Water and **Fire**. In *The Blue Jar*, Helena, the daughter of a nobleman, travels the globe searching for the perfect blue jar, a symbol of her love for a young merchant seaman who rescued her from a burning ship and sailed with her for nine days. After they were both rescued, her father paid him to disappear to the other hemisphere, prompting Helena's need to keep moving to keep pace with her lover's ship, a reflection of her own on the other side of the globe. Finally she finds her perfect blue jar, 'as deep as a deep secret', and asks for her heart to be placed in it when she dies, so 'all shall be blue around me'.

Sea myths abound in the literature of sea-faring nations. Shakespeare's *The Tempest* even contributed the term 'sea-change' to the English language, to imply a complete transformation, as in the effect of the sea on the body of the King of Naples expressed in Ariel's song to Ferdinand, the king's son:

> Full fathom five thy father lies;
> Of his bones are coral made;
> Those are pearls that were his eyes;
> Nothing of him doth fade
> But doth suffer a sea-change
> Into something rich and strange
> Sea nymphs hourly ring his knell.

The *Mermaid of Zennor* is one of my favourite Cornish sea legends of all those my Cornish mother told us as children. It's the tale of a mermaid who falls in love with one of the young men of the tiny coastal hamlet of Zennor, after hearing him sing in the church choir. He eventually joins her under the ocean. It's said their voices can still be heard above the roar of the waves crashing against the rugged cliffs, although a local author tells me the voices belong to a couple of sea lions. A pew in the church bears a fine carving of the mermaid to this day. Zennor and its various sea legends have attracted countless visitors throughout the years, including famous literary figures of the early twentieth century, such as DH Lawrence and Virginia Woolf.

Deep Chords

Within the Five Elements, **Water** is the darkest, the most **Yin**, the most secretive, silent, the most hidden, and because of that, the most tantalising. The earliest forms of life were aquatic creatures. We floated in amniotic fluid in our mother's womb. So **Water** hits some deep chords in us, memories we cannot reach, a place where we want to hide in moments of trauma and fear.

To experience another aspect of **Water**, pick up a large seashell next time you walk along a beach, and hold it close to your ear to hear the roar of the ocean. This is also a way of reminding ourselves that the ears are sound chambers. In addition, they control our equilibrium – and much more. In the southern states of America, the expression 'I hear you', means, 'I understand you'. In the past ten years, I have had interesting experiences with three medical doctors suffering from tinnitus in different parts of the world. In all cases, the doctors were suffering from overload, their ears were literally overloaded with their patients' problems.

One of them happened to love playing the violin. In addition to my treatments, I suggested he should take long baths and listen to the sort of music (Mozart) that not only soothed him, but actually helped to neutralise the sound in his ears. After a few weeks, he told me this was the first relief he had experienced for months. In the second case, I felt that the ear problem reflected the disharmony in the doctor's marriage, and she agreed. In the third case, Dr Carien Wijnen, a Dutch doctor based in Berlin, a fine singer who also teaches singing to groups, told me she realised the problem was caused by 'pushing too much, by trying to be too perfect'. She described this as 'typical Type A behaviour' of the sort that prompts heart attacks. A natural healer in Holland told her 'When you have tinnitus, you don't hear your heart, there's a block of energy and circulation.' This was a wake-up call for Wijnen, especially as music is the essence of her medical practice.

Sound and Movement

We all know the soothing effects of beautiful music, and the fragmenting effects of, say, noise pollution in our busiest cities, or heavy metal rock, and how both can affect behaviour patterns. In his work *Die Welt is Klang (The World is Sound)* author Joachim-Ernst Berendt describes experiments testing the way plants react to different forms of music. They grow towards speakers playing Bach: they curl around speakers playing Ravi Shanker: they grow away from speakers playing heavy metal rock. Not surprisingly, ear specialists on both sides of the Atlantic tell me that exposure to heavy metal rock, and over-usage of the walkman, is prompting more and more hearing problems among teenagers.

Beethoven composed one of his finest works when he was deaf – his ninth symphony – containing Schiller's *Ode to Joy* – a fine example of **Water** (his deafness) finding an expression through music in harmony with **Fire** (*Ode to Joy*).

We can also appreciate the extraordinary experience of Hitari Oe, son of Nobel prize-winning author Kenzaburo Oe of Japan. The young Oe was born brain damaged, but was exposed to music from a very young age because of his mother's love of the classics. He was also exposed to the sounds of nature, especially birds. The first word he uttered was 'bird', and he grew up to become a fine classical composer. Many of his works are available on CD.

Another **Metal–Water–Wood–Fire** example comes to mind through the experience of the inspiring Helen Keller, who was born blind (eyes = **Wood**) and deaf (ears = **Water**). Her teacher, Annie Sullivan, first broke through to the wildly uncontrollable Helen as a child by turning on a tap full force, holding the child's hand under it, and then writing the letters of the word **Water** on her palm (skin-to-skin contact = **Metal**). This breakthrough was the first step in direct communication that led to other forms of communication and, ultimately, speech (**Fire**).

Still Waters

Water controls our bones, our scaffolding, our inner structure. This is why bathing in the ocean, in salt water, has been found to hasten the recovery of people suffering from damaged or broken bones.

In Chinese Medicine, the Kidneys hold our essence, our **Jing**, controlling our ancestral energy, our internal source of vitality, of **Ki** and the milestones of our reproductive cycles, from puberty to menopause. In modern terms, it controls our genes, our DNA. **Water** also controls our hair, as well as our bones and marrow, which is why chemotherapy hits **Water** so forcefully, often resulting in a loss of hair, early menopause in women and memory loss.

We deplete our **Water** energy not just by overworking, but by giving too much of our 'essence', or **Jing**, especially those of us in the healing profession or some other vocation. We run the risk of healer's burn-out, or 'compassion fatigue'. Remember my case study of David the veterinarian? He burnt himself out by running all over London at all hours to see to his furry patients, compounded by the fact that he was using work overload to avoid dealing with his father's death.

In my Zen Shiatsu practice, I have also discovered that the **Water** meridians, especially the Kidney meridian, hold the deepest memories, forgotten memories. Sometimes just a simple stretch or subtle touch can bring these memories floating spontaneously to the surface, like something gently loosened from the ocean floor. The memories can range from past dreams to deeply submerged memories of childhood sexual abuse.

Bones and Idioms

Our bones, our marrow, our scaffolding symbolise the most hidden but tangible part of our bodies. Think of the number of expressions in different languages where 'bones' imply something very deep and basic. In English, 'I feel something in my bones', or 'I feel something in my water' implies a deeply intuitive sense of knowing what is going on or about to happen, but is as yet unseen or unknown. Bones and fear come together in a number of German expressions: *ihm steckt die Angst in den Knochen* ('fear is stuck in his/her bones – he/she is scared stiff'.) 'Pass the Bone', meaning 'to share your knowledge', is an example of current American campus slang I picked up off the Internet. In Russian, 'If your bones remain, the flesh will grow on them again' (*biili bii kosti a myaso narastyet*), meaning, 'if you have a solid foundation, you can always build on it'. In Italian, *le ossa rotte* (literally, 'to have broken bones') means 'to be dead tired'.

Sacred Waters

Water (a spiral) is a frequent symbol in Hopi art and graphics, for a very obvious reason. It is scarce in America's dry south-west, and thus sacred. Those of us who have experienced the desperation of a severe drought well know the sanctity of a single drop of water. Similar water symbols appear in Aboriginal stone art. But even in countries where there are no shortages of water (as in Britain), wells and springs often became sacred sites. Sacred Celtic springs in Cornwall were used by the earliest Christian hermits as places of worship, appropriately, because local people were long accustomed to cherishing and visiting those sites for healings, predictions and inspiration.

Mythic traditions surround Cornwall's countless sacred wells to this day. St Nun's Well is supposed to cure the insane. The effect of a good dunking in icy spring water – or raging sea water – has long been thought of as a shock tactic to cure the insane, and shock is associated with the **Water** element. On a lighter note, the first of a newly married couple to drink the waters of St Keyne's Well is supposed to rule the home from that day on. Anyone who alters a Holy Well risks drowning, according to Robert Hunt, author of *Customs and Superstitions from Cornish Folklore*. Beyond superstition, sacred or healing waters, wells or rivers link many of the world's religions, from the Ganges beloved of Hindus to the Jordan of Judaism and Christianity, and the healing springs of Bernadette of Lourdes. From the Jewish *mikvah* to the Christian baptismal font, water is the symbol of transformation.

The related and often sacred symbols and colours of the water element are common to many of the desert cultures. The Tuareg men of the South Sahara are dramatic figures in their traditional attire and blue headscarves, with just enough of a gap left for their eyes. Blue = water and blue = cool, so we discover another grand expression of it in the huge, blue mosaic Babylonian temple structure known as the Gate of Ishtar, now housed in the Pergamon museum, Berlin. The shimmering, cooling effect of this massive structure could probably be seen for miles as an enduring symbol of worship, of the goddess who brings sustenance and relief to the parched throats and relentless glare of the surrounding desert.

Chilly Tales

On a milder note, those of us from British backgrounds are well accustomed to the cold, northern, wintry aspects of **Water**, to endless chills, freezing cold bathrooms and dampness and darkness falling early in the day. Inherent in the British mind is the notion that exposing yourself to cold and razor sharp winds, and a good drenching by sea spray during a winter walk along a craggy cliff top, somehow builds character and strength. Icy fresh air is the ultimate cure-all. Fling your windows open to the elements if you're sick in bed. There's something slightly sinful, indulgent, about being too warm, too comfortable. Two stories come to mind.

When my godmother Marie Exelby had tuberculosis at the end of the 1940s in Cornwall, the treatment at that time involved daily exposure to cold sea air in a sanatorium built on the rugged cliffs. 'Streptomyacin was saved for members of the armed forces returning from the war,' she said. 'There wasn't enough for us.' Later, she underwent surgery to remove most of her lungs. A teacher, Marie managed her own rehabilitation by practising the sort of upper body stretches, rotations and exercises she taught to her schoolchildren. Today, Marie's a feisty octogenarian determined to see the twenty-first century.

As a young woman in the early 1930s, my mother experienced Black Water fever (when malaria affects the kidneys) in Zambia (then Northern Rhodesia). She never got over the horror of urinating black liquid. The cure in those days was to dunk patients in bathtubs of freezing cold water. She never got over the horror of that experience, either! Dunking was something of a shock tactic, no longer in general use.

For most of us, **Water** is somewhat less dramatic, winter being a time when we withdraw a little, replenish our fires, reflect, follow intellectual pursuits, read Russian novels. Dr Oliver Sacks, an obsessive swimmer, says he does all his thinking in the water. I am also reminded of the calming, balancing effect swimming had on the volatile and controversial Australian pianist David Helfgott, whose story was told in the book *I Love you with all my Heart* by his wife Gillian, and in the movie *Shine*.

A Pinch of Salt

In the countries of the far north, excessively salty foods like salted fish are, of course, more culturally common and appropriate than in the south. Imagine eating salted herrings for breakfast in the tropics. You'd die of thirst. And yet, invite someone who lives in a hot climate for dinner and notice the amount of salt they shake on the food you've prepared. Don't feel insulted: they'll sweat it out when they go home.

Salt is scouring, cleansing. Toss it in a pot of near-boiling water and watch the water boil and churn rapidly. Toss salt on red wine to soak it up the instant you spill it on your best white tablecloth, a great example of **Water** controlling **Fire**. Toss a handful of chunky sea salt down your blocked drain, with a pan of boiling water, to clear debris. Sumo wrestlers toss salt in the air and all over their bodies in purification rituals before they fight. Are we also purifying the air when we toss salt over our shoulder for luck after we spill it on the dinner table? Salt plays densely serious roles in our languages. In English, 'to rub salt in the wounds' means to add to someone's pain. We talk about someone being 'worth their salt'. The English word 'salary' is derived from salt, dating back to the days when people were paid salt money. In Russian 'Before you make a friend, you must eat a bushel of salt with him/her' (*chtobii oozhat cheloveka nado s him pood soli siest*). The word salty in English, meaning risqué, probably comes from the association of the word salt to imply a sailor.

Water also gives us one of our most basic expressions in English and German 'to piss your pants with fear' (*sich vor Angst in die Hosen machen.*)

Art and Fear

One of my most intense experiences of the **Water** element was at a disturbing exhibition entitled 'Angst and Inuit Art' at Toronto's Art Gallery of Ontario at the end of 1997. Picture a small, dimly lit room at the top of a spiral staircase apart from the main gallery. Spotlights illuminated various shapes and figures with mouths silently screaming, eyes wide open, in a range of textures from porous whalebone, antler and ivory, to black soapstone. Exhibition notes described some of the sculptors' battles with manic depression and alcoholism, and included a statement from an Inuit elder:

> Fear is an emotion that traditional Inuit experience daily. We do not believe, we fear. We fear the weather spirit of the Earth, that we must fight against to wrest our food from land and sea. We fear death and hunger in cold snow huts. We fear the sickness that we must meet with daily all around us; not death, but the suffering.

Black Thoughts

Cultures with strong historic links to the sea often have blue or black in their national flags or colours. Think of Greece, with its distinctive blue

Inuit artist Menasie Akpaliapik expresses many aspects of the Water element in his disturbing work 'Respecting the Circle' in whalebone, stone and horn. His work is part of a permanent exhibition 'Angst and Inuit Art' at Toronto's Art Gallery of Ontario. (© Manasie Akpaliapik, AGO, Toronto)

and white flag; or Cornwall, with its black and white flag – the flag of St Pirran, the patron saint of tin mining, so the flag combines Cornwall's most characteristic activities, fishing and mining.

Writing about black brings the story of St Meinrad, the fifteenth-century patron saint of Einsiedeln, Switzerland, to mind. After he was murdered by a couple of thieves, his two blackbirds hovered above their heads so the townspeople knew who they were. The story echoes an African myth that two birds will always fly above the heads of thieves and murderers. The two blackbirds have been a symbol of Einsiedeln ever since. And appropriately so, because the monastery founded by St Meinrad is the home of one of the world's sacred Black Madonnas, a site of pilgrimage for the sick and lamed, for decades.

In the West we often associate black with mourning, funerals, and widowhood, depending on the culture. Or, it is used culturally to make women invisible, as in the habits of some religious orders, and as in the *chador* of countries practising Muslem fundamentalism. Depending on the style, black is dramatic and formal in evening attire, but if worn during the day, can be your way of saying, 'I need distance'. It is also a dramatic statement made by designers like Armani, who wears black constantly, and can be spotted in a crowd. It's a neutral shade favoured by many referees in football. Late nineteenth-century British artist Aubrey Beardsley, best known for his flamboyant black-and-white – and some colour – illustrations for Oscar Wilde and Edgar Allan Poe, worked in a black room by the light of a flickering candle, for its mystical and magical effects.

However, the word black is also used negatively in a number of languages ('blackmail', 'blacklist', 'blackout' in English); similar expressions in German include *Schwarzarbeit* ('illegal work'), and *Schwarzfahrer* (joyrider). In Arabic, the expression *Zai el Zift* (Black as tar) can be used to describe a bad person or situation.

Politically correct consciousness has encouraged us to re-examine the casual ways in which we use these words in English and German in particular, because of perpetuating stereotypes (black = negative/white = positive).

Afterthoughts

Don't think too much. Wait a few days and see which of the Elements and images and sayings and colours linger in your mind, and why. Once you have applied the assorted associations of the Law to yourself in all kinds of ways, you will find it much easier to apply to others – more so if you happen to be in the healing profession.

Just let everything sink in. Use yourself as a laboratory.

And remember that marvellous Zen expression, 'If enlightenment isn't around your feet, where will you look?'

Notes

Preface
1. 'The Hippocratic Wars', in *New York Times* magazine, 26 June 1998.

Introduction
1. Home Box Office
2. 'Despite the Despair of Depression, Few Men Seek Treatment, in the *New York Times*, 30 December 1997.

Chapter 1
1. *Painting by Numbers — A Scientific Guide to Art*, by Komar, Melamid and Wypijewski.
2. The *Independent*, London 17 September 1997.
3. 17 February 1998.

Chapter 2
1. 'The Midsummer Bonfire Ceremony, by Ann Trevenan Jenkin, in *Cornish World* Number 6, September 1995.
2. *The Nordic Elements: Fire, Water, Ice, Air, Silence, Darkness*, by Henrietta Hulten.
3. *The Complete Medicinal Herbal*, by Penelope Ody.
4. Survey in the *International Herald Tribune*, late 1980s.
5. 'China's Missing Girls,' in the *New York Times*, 30 October 1997.
6. 'China officially lifts filter on staggering pollution data', in the *New York Times*, 14 June 1998.
7. National Public Radio News, 27 August 1997.

Chapter 7
1. *The English Patient*, by Michael Ondaatje, Vintage edition, p. 16.
2. *International Herald Tribune*, 6–7 April 1996.
3. 'At 50 – Taking the Stage (and a Risk) Alone', in the *New York Times*, 18 January 1998.
4. PBS TV, 10 February 1998.
5. *Colour Psychology and Colour Therapy*, by Vassily Kandinsky.

Afterword and Addresses

My appreciation to the following for their help:

The Winiker family in Switzerland for *Fasnacht* insights. The Berens family in Germany.

Art Museums

Asian Art Museum (Hanni Forrester), Golden Gate Park, San Francisco, CA 94118 (web site: www.asianart.org). 'Flowers and Birds of the Twelve Months' Yamamoto Soken, act. 1683–1706, Edo period, late seventeenth century, pair of six-fold screens, ink and colours on silk (The Avery Brundage Collection, 1997).

Art Gallery of Ontario (Fellicia Cukier), 317 Dundas St West, Toronto, Ontario M5T 1G4 Canada (email: Felicia Cukier@ago.net). 'Respecting the Circle' Menasie Akpaliapik (Canadian Inuit), from exhibit entitled 'Angst and Inuit Art', whalebone, ivory, dark grey stone, antler, baleen, rust stone, horn (Gift of Samuel and Esther Sarick, Toronto, 1996).

Philadelphia Museum of Art (Katleen Ryan), Box 7646, Philadelphia PA 19101–7646. 'The Six Elements', c. 1928, Rene Magritte (Lousie and Walter Arensberg Collection).

Media

National Media (June Botha), PO Box 1802, Cape Town, South Africa 8000. Tel.: 021 406 2281 (South-easter photos).

Chatelaine, Maclean Hunter Building, 777 Bay St, Toronto, Ontario M5W 1A7, Canada. Tel.: 416 596 5425.

Events

Stockholm, Cultural Capital of Europe 1998 (Europas Kulturhuvudstad '98), Box 163 98, S–103 27 Stockholm (Fire photo: Lennart Nystrom. Ice photo: Jan Jordan. Tel.: 070 622 42 98.

Artists and Photographers
Jessica Higgins. Email: yoohoo@thing.net.

Minh, Karen Greathouse, Nancy Scanlan, He Yan Wu, Marina Dodis, via the author.

Schools
Academy of Oriental Medicine at Austin, Village Center, 2700 West Anderson Lane, Austin, Texas 78757, USA. Tel.: 512 454 1188. Web site: www.aoma.edu/newsite.

Association: American Oriental Bodywork Therapy Association, Laurel Oak Corporate Center, #408, 1010 Haddonfield-Berlin Rd, Voorhees NJ 08043. Tel.: 609 782 1616. Email: aobta@prodigy.net. Website: www.healthy.net/AOBTA.

Canada
Shiatsu Centre (Tetsuro Saito), 1069 Bathurst St, Toronto, Ontario, Canada M5R 3GB. Tel.: 416 534 1149.

Shiatsu School of Canada, 547 College St, Toronto, Ontario, Canada M6G 1A9. Tel.: 416 323 1818.

United Kingdom
Shiatsu College London, Unit 62, Pall Mall Deposit, 126–128 Barlby Rd, London W10 6BL. Tel.: 0181 987 0208.

Germany
Bernhard Ruhla, Helmholzstr 2, 01069, Dresden. Tel.: 0351/4715136.

Tianzi-Zentrum fur Chinesische Medizin: Matthias Wiek, Brunnenstr 181, 10119 Berlin. Tel.: 03322 238088.

Shaitsu-Zentrum Edith Storch: Oranienstrr 163, 10969 Berlin-Kreuzberg. Tel.: 030 615 1686.

Schule fur Shiatsu Berlin Düsseldorf: (Berlin) Elli Mann-Langhof, Wilhelmsaue 11, 10715 Berlin. Tel.: 030 873 4404; (Düsseldorf) Heide

Kuhl-buro: Katharinna De Fries Carmenstr 3, 40549 Düsseldorf. Tel.: 0211 55 81 3300.

Schule fur Shiatsu Hamburg: Wilfried Rappenecker, Oelkersallee 33, 22769 Hamburg. Tel.: 040 430 1885.

Association: Gesellschaft fur Shiatsu in Deutschland (Shaitsu Society in Germany): Marion Hennemann, KunoldStr 26, 34131 Kassel. Tel.: 0561 392 84.

Switzerland

Erika Bringold, Shiatsu-Padagogin: Trottenwiesenstr 19b, CH–8404 Winterthur. Tel.: 052 242 5678.

Christin Stalder, HOLLA, Unt. Batterieweg 46, CH–4053 Basel. Tel.: 061 361 1566.

Association: Shaitsu Gesellschaft Schweiz (SGS) (Shiatsu Society Switzerland), Secretariat, Postfach 350, CH–5430 Wettingen 1.

Other Useful Addresses

The Achromatopsia Network: PO Box 214, Berkeley CA 94701–0214. Tel.: 510 540 700. Email: Futterman@achromat.org. Website: http://www.achromat.org.

Architecture and Design

Renato Severino, 6 Upland Rd, Greenwich Connecticut USA. Tel.: 203 629 8386.

Andre Studer, Nussbaumstr 1, CH–8044 Gockhausen, Switzerland. Tel.: 01 821 0217.

Sophie Keir, The Creative Edge, 295 Bowery, New York NY 10003. Tel.: 212 260 2267.

(Feng Shui) Annie Grey, 2706 Windswept Cove, #3, Austin Texas 78745. Tel.: 512 891 0591.

Languages

Alighta Averbukh. Website: www.io.com/~alighta.

Gaye Kynoch, Eve Berens, Ute Schwarzer and Karimah Tarazi, via the author.

Bibliography

Arts, Culture, History and Rituals

Apperson, G.L., *The Wordsworth Dictionary of Proverbs*, Herts, UK: Wordsworth Editions Ltd 1993

Aria, Barbara, with Gon, Russel Eng, *The Spirit of the Chinese Character*, San Francisco, CA, USA: Chronicle Books 1992

Beckett, Sister Wendy, *Sister Wendy's Grand Tour: Discovering Europe's Great Art*, New York: Stewart, Tabori and Chang (division of US Media Holdings Inc) 1996

Blakemore, Frances, *Japanese Design Through Textile Patterns*, New York: Weatherhill Inc 1978

Bock, Hanna, *Einsiedeln, Das Kloster Und Seine Geschichte*, Zurich: Silva-Verlag 1991

Callan, Anthea, *Techniques of the Impressionists*, New Jersey: Chartwell Books 1997

Chevalier, Jean and Alain Gheerbrant, *The Penguin Dictionary of Symbols*, London: Penguin Books Ltd 1996

Do You know Cornwall? Guidebook, Redruth Cornwall: Tor Mark Press 1993

Ellis, Peter Berresford, *The Cornish Saints*, Penryn, Cornwall: Tor Mark Press 1992

Evans, Ivor H., *The Wordsworth Dictionary of Phrase & Fable*, London: Wordsworth Editions 1993

Funk, Wilfred, *Word Origins: An Exploration and History of Words and Language*, New York: Wing Books 1950

Frazer, James G. *The Golden Bough: The Roots of Religion and Folklore*, New York: Gramercy Books 1981

Gaskell, G.A., *Dictionary of All Scriptures and Myths*, New York: Gramercy Books 1981

Gibson, Clare, *Signs and Symbols: An Illustrated Guide to their Meaning and Origins*, New York: Saraband/Barnes & Noble Inc 1966

Grun, Bernard, *The Timetables of History: A Horizontal Linkage of People and Events*, New York: Touchstone/Simon & Schuster 1982

Holzherr, Abbot Georg, *Einsiedeln Abbey Church*, Munich: Verlag Schnell & Steiner 1994

Humphreys, Christmas, *The Buddhist Way*, London: Diamond Books 1996

Hunt Robert, *Cornish Folk-lore*, Penryn, Cornwall: Tor Mark Press 1992

Hunt Robert, *Customs and Superstitions from Cornish Folklore* Penryn, Cornwall: Tor Mark Press 1991

Jayakar, Pupul, *The Earth Mother, Legends, Goddesses and Ritual Arts of India*, San Francisco: Harper & Row 1990

Komar, Vitaly (ed), **Melamid (Alexander) and Wypijewski, Joann** (ed), *Painting by Numbers, Komar and Melamid's Scientific Guide to Art*, New York: Farrar, Straus and Giroux, 1997

Kornfield, Jack (ed), *Teachings of the Buddha*, Boston, Mass: Shambala Books 1993

Knappert, Jan, *African Mythology*, London: Diamond Books 1995

McAlpine, Helen and William, *Japanese Tales and Legends*, Oxford: Oxford University Press 1993

Mish, Frederick C., *The Merriam-Webster New Book of Word Histories*, Springfield, Mass: Merriam-Webster Inc 1991

Muramara Norikazu, *Japanese Folktales*, Tokyo: Yohan Publications Inc 1994

Pomar, Maria Teresa, *El Día de los Muertos: The Life of the Dead in Mexican Art*, Fort Worth, Texas: Modern Art Museum of Fort Worth 1995

Roberts, J.M., *The Penguin History of the World*, London: Penguin Group 1990

Severino, Renato, *Meta-Realism in Architecture in Quest of the Ideal City*, Milan: Idea Books 1995

Shlain, Leonard, *Art and Physics: Parallel Visions in Space, Time and Light*, New York: William Morrow and Co. Inc 1991

Slessor, Catherine, *The Art of Aubrey Beardsley*, London: Quintet Publishing, London 1989

Taube, Karl, *Aztec and Maya Myths*, Austin, Texas: University of Texas Press 1995

Tisellius, Henric and Henrietta Hulten (eds), *The Orange Pages: Program Catalogue for Stockholm, Stockholm*: The City of Stockholm 1998

Trachsler, Beat and Jane Roberts, *Basler Fasnacht: For Insiders and Outsiders*, Basel CH: GS-Verlag 1992

Walker, Barbara, *The Women's Encyclopedia of Myths and Secrets*, New Jersey: Castle Books, Edison 1996

Weatherhill, Craig and Paul Devereux, *Myths and Legends of Cornwall*, Wilmslow, Cheshire UK: Sigma Leisure Books 1998

Westwood, Jennifer (ed), *Mysterious Places: The World's Unexplained Symbolic Sites, Ancient Cities and Lost Lands*, New York: Barnes & Noble 1997

Yoshida, Shoya, *Folk Art*, Osaka Japan: Hoikusha Publishing Co. 1992

Yu, Leslie Tseng-Tseng, *Chinese Painting in Four Seasons – A Manual of Aesthetics & Techniques*, Engelwood Cliffs, New Jersey: Prentice-Hall 1981

Art Museum Publications
René Magritte, Montreal, Quebec: Musée des Beaux Arts 1996 *Tomb Treasures from China – The Buried Art of Ancient Xi'an*, Asian Art Museum of San Francisco and Kimbell Art Museum, Fort Worth, Texas 1994

Colour
Andrews, Ted, *How to Heal with Colour*, St Paul, Minn: Llewellyn Publications 1992

Chijiwa, Hideaki, *Colour Harmony: A Guide to Creative Colour Combinations*, Rockport, Mass: Rockport Publishers/North Light Books 1987

Goethe, J.W. von (theory of colour), *Goethe: Collected Works in English*, New York: Suhrkamp 1988

Ivie, Lana, *Lessons in Colour Meditation*, Jerome, Arizona: Luminary Press 1984

Wauters, Ambika and Thompson, Gerry, *Principles of Colour Healing*, Thorsons, Harper Collins 1997

Feng Shui
Lip, Evelyn, *Feng Shui for the Home*, Torrance CA: Heian International 1990

Wydra, Nancilee, *Feng Shui: The Book of Cures*, Chicago: Contemporary Books 1996

Wydra, Nancilee, *Feng Shui in the Garden*, Chicago: Contemporary Books 1997

Eastern Medicine
Beinfield Harriet and Korngold, Efrem, *Between Heaven and Earth: A Guide to Chinese Medicine*, New York: Ballantine Books 1991

Beresford-Cooke, Carola, *Shiatsu Theory and Practice*, London & New York: Churchill Livingstone 1996

Connelly, Dianne M., *Traditional Acupuncture: The Law of the Five Elements*, Columbia, Maryland: The Centre for Traditional Acupuncture 1975

Kaptchuk, Ted J., *The Web That Has No Weaver: Understanding Chinese Medicine*, New York: Congdon & Weed Inc 1983

Maciocia, Giovanni, *The Foundations of Chinese Medicine*, New York & London: Churchill Livingstone 1989

Masunaga, Shizuto with Wataru Ohashi, *Zen Shiatsu: How to Harmonise Yin & Yang for Better Health*, Japan Publications (Distributed by Harper & Row USA) 1977

Matsumoto, Kiiko and Stephen Birch, *Hara Diagnosis: Reflections on the Sea*, Brookline Mass, USA: Paradigm Publications 1988

Matsumoto, Kiiko and Stephen Birch, *Five Elements and Ten Stems*, Brookline Mass, USA: Paradigm Publications 1983

Monte, Tom (and the editors of *East West Natural Health*), *World Medicine – The East West Guide to Healing Your Body*, Jeremy P. Tarcher/Perigee 1993

Rappenecker, Wilfred, *Fünf Element Und Zwölf Meridiane: Ein Handbuch Für Shiatsu, Akupunktur Und Körperarbeit*, Waldeck: Felicitas Hubner Verlag 1996

Williams, Tom, *The Complete Illustrated Guide to Chinese Medicine, A Comprehensive System for Health and Fitness*, Element Books/ Barnes & Noble 1996

Western Medicine and Environmental Medicine

Caldicott, Helen, *If You Love This Planet: A Plan to Heal the Earth*, New York: WW Norton 1992

Carson, Rachel, *Silent Spring*, Greenwich, Conn USA: Fawcett Crest Books 1962

Chadwick, J. and Mann, W.N. (eds), *Hippocratic Writings*, London: Penguin Books 1983

Korda, Michael, *Man to Man, Surviving Prostate Cancer*, New York: Vintage Books 1997

Lust, John, *The Herb Book*, New York: Bantam Books 1974

Mann, John, *Murder, Magic and Medicine*, Oxford UK: Oxford University Press 1992

Morgeli, Christoph, *The Museum of the History of Medicine of the University of Zurich*, Zurich: Institute and Museum of the History of Medicine 1994

Needleman, Herbert L. and Landrigan, Philip J., *Raising Children Toxic Free*, New York: Avon Books 1994

Ody, Penelope, *The Complete Medicinal Herbal*, New York: Dorling Kindersley 1993

O'Malley, Charles D.O. and Saunders, JB de CM (eds), *Leonardo da Vinci on the Human Body*, New York:Wing Books 1982

Sacks, Oliver, *An Anthropologist on Mars*, New York: Alfred A. Knopf 1995

Sacks, Oliver, *The Island of the Colorblind*, New York: Alfred A. Knopf 1997

Steingraber, Sandra, *Living Downstream: An Ecologist Looks at Cancer and the Environment*, Reading, Mass USA: A Merloyd Lawrence Book (Addison Wesley Publishing Company) 1997

Stocker, Midge (ed), *Confronting Cancer, Confronting Change: New Perspectives on Women and Cancer*, Chicago USA: Third Side Press 1993

World's Kitchens

Creber, Ann and King, Elisabeth, *The World's Finest Food – 180 Classic Recipes From Around the World*, New York: Welcome Book 1994

Hooker, Monique, Jamet and Richardson, Tracie, *Cooking with the Seasons: A Year in My Kitchen*, New York: Henry Holt and Co 1997

Mascetti, Manuela Dunn and Borthwick, Arunima, *Food for the Spirit, Seasonal Vegetarian Recipes to Warm the Kitchen and Nourish the Soul*, Rodale, New York: Daybreak Books 1998

Pitchford, Paul, *Healing with Whole Foods: Oriental Traditions and Modern Nutrition*, Berkeley, CA: North Atlantic Books 1993

Sahni, Julie, *Classic Indian Cooking*, New York: William Morrow & Co 1980

Style, Sue, A Taste of Switzerland, New York: William Morrow & Co 1992

Temelie, Barbara, *Ernährung nach den Fünf Elementen*, Sulzberg: Joy Verlag 1995

Fiction, Poetry and Plays

Capote, Truman, *The Grass Harp*, New York: Vintage/Random House 1995

Dinesen, Isak, 'The Blue Jar' from *Tales of Wisdom, One Hundred Modern Parables*, edited by Howard Schwartz, New York: Crescent Books/ Random House 1991

Frye, Northrup (ed), *The Pelican Shakespeare: The Tempest*, New York: Penguin Books 1970

Gibran, Kahlil, *The Eye of the Prophet*, Berkeley, Ca: Frog 1995

Gogol, Nikolai, *The Overcoat and the Nose*, New York: Penguin Books 1995

Ibsen, Hendrik, *Four Plays: Ghosts, An Enemy of the People, the Wild Duck and Hedda Gabler*, Holt, Rhinehart and Winston Inc 1970

Keller, Helen, *The Story of My Life*, New York: Signet/Penguin Books 1988

Oe, Kenzaburo, *Teach Us to Outgrow Our Madness*, New York: Grove Press 1977

Ondaatje, Michael, *The English Patient*, New York: Vintage International/ Random House 1993

Schneider, Robert, *Brother of Sleep*, Woodstock, New York: The Overlook Press 1996 (Deutsch: *Schlafes Bruder*, Leipzig: Reclam Verlag 1994)

Singer, Isaac Bashevis, *Gimpel the Fool and Other Stories*, New York: The Noonday Press/Farrar Strauss and Giroux 1993

Stevens, John, ed, *Lotus Moon – The Poetry of the Buddhist Nun Rengetsu*, New York: Weatherhill 1994

Yarmolinsky, Avrahm, ed, *The Portable Chekov*, New York: Penguin Books 1995

Yen Mah, Adeline, *Falling Leaves*, London: Penguin Books 1997

Index